STOP HIGH-STAKES TESTING

STOP HIGH-STAKES TESTING

An Appeal to America's Conscience

Dale D. Johnson,
Bonnie Johnson,
Stephen J. Farenga,
and
Daniel Ness

ROWMAN & LITTLEFIELD PUBLISHERS, INC.

Lanham • Boulder • New York • Toronto • Plymouth, UK

ROWMAN & LITTLEFIELD PUBLISHERS, INC.

Published in the United States of America
by Rowman & Littlefield Publishers, Inc.
A wholly owned subsidiary of The Rowman & Littlefield Publishing Group, Inc.
4501 Forbes Boulevard, Suite 200, Lanham, Maryland 20706
www.rowmanlittlefield.com

Estover Road
Plymouth PL6 7PY
United Kingdom

British Library Cataloguing in Publication Information Available

Library of Congress Cataloging-in-Publication Data:

Stop high-stakes testing : an appeal to America's conscience / Dale Johnson . . . [et al.].
    p. cm.
  Includes bibliographical references and index.
  ISBN-13: 978-0-7425-5937-0 (cloth : alk. paper)
  ISBN-10: 0-7425-5937-8 (cloth : alk. paper)
  ISBN-13: 978-0-7425-5938-7 (pbk. : alk. paper)
  ISBN-10: 0-7425-5938-6 (pbk. : alk. paper)
    1. Educational tests and measurements—United States. 2. Educational accountability—
United States. 3. Educational equalization—United States. 4. Children with social
disabilities—United States. I. Johnson, Dale.
  LB3051.S856 2008
  371.26'20973—dc22   2007008961

Printed in the United States of America

∞™ The paper used in this publication meets the minimum requirements of American
National Standard for Information Sciences—Permanence of Paper for Printed Library
Materials, ANSI/NISO Z39.48-1992.

Contents

Foreword

---

*S*TOP *HIGH-STAKES TESTING: AN APPEAL TO AMERICA'S CONSCIENCE* critiques today's unprecedented reliance on high-stakes testing in our public schools. The negative effects on students, teachers, parents, administrators, and others are documented through historical data, supportive research, and interviews with children and their teachers. Consequences of chronic racism, rooted in the slavery era, and classism, rooted in poverty, are examined.

This volume should bring high-stakes testing to the forefront of political discussion. The authors present a convincing case that documents the inequalities in educational communities that serve the *included* and *excluded* classes. Readers are called upon to examine the roles of tutoring programs and are asked if those who need the most help from these programs are receiving it. Descriptions of programs available to affluent youth serve as a model to holistically assist children of poverty.

Throughout *Stop High-Stakes Testing: An Appeal to America's Conscience*, Johnson, Johnson, Farenga, and Ness present sensible solutions to the problems exacerbated by high-stakes testing. The closing pages delineate **what we all know** should, can, and must be done to rid our schools of a stacked deck against children of poverty. Readers of this book will be provided with a new deck of cards to shuffle into a hand that will help our children reach their potential.

Delores B. Malcolm
Former Director of Teaching and
Learning Support, St. Louis Public Schools
Past President, International Reading Association

Acknowledgments

W E ARE INDEBTED TO THE TEACHERS AND STUDENTS across the country who shared their school experiences with us. We thank Ms. Mary Simons who gave freely of her time to share valuable observations, and Dr. Delores Malcolm for her insightful Foreword. Special thanks to literacy research students at Dowling College who conducted many of the Long Island interviews contained in these pages. We are appreciative of Dowling College administrators and faculty who provided the release time so that we could engage in this study. The expertise and good natures of Alan McClare, executive editor, and Alex Masulis, editorial assistant at Rowman & Littlefield, encouraged us throughout the project. We also acknowledge the professional work and contributions of Elaine McGarraugh, production editor, and Veronica Jurgena, copy editor.

Introduction

R ODENT AND COCKROACH INFESTATIONS in school buildings. Urinals that leak and do not flush. No hot water. More than 200 health violations cited by the state Office of Public Health. An *A* awarded to the state by *Education Week* (2006) in the *Standards and Accountability* category.

Snow on classroom bookshelves in a room not warm enough to melt it. No school library. A computer lab with no working computers. Fighting and gang violence—the MS13 Salvadorians and the Bloods. Ceilings leaking and falling down, bathroom stall doors broken or missing, holes in walls, peeling paint. An *A* awarded to the state by *Education Week* (2006) in the *Standards and Accountability* category.

Conditions in the first paragraph exist in a rural Louisiana parish; those in the second paragraph are found in the New York City metro area. In June 2006, the Union Parish (Louisiana) School Board was given a notice by the Office of Public Health; it had recorded 19 pages of violations in the public schools. A sanitary director for the region noted, "You may have 25 to 30 kids go in and use the urinal and it only flushes one time and then it don't flush all of it" (Lezama 2006). Union Parish school superintendent Judy Mabry commented, "We're working as hard as we can. We've got some old facilities, and no money has been put into these facilities for years." Mabry predicted that all of the violations would not be corrected. "There's just too much," she said (Morrison 2006). The Union Parish violations are not peculiar to that district. In the previous year the Louisiana Office of Public Health found 65 health violations in the Franklin Parish public schools.

The accountability movement with its unprincipled high-stakes testing policies does not consider the conditions in which some pupils are expected to learn. Adults who do not work in these foul conditions seem unaware of their existence or unmoved by them. In response to the *A* in *Standards and Accountability* bestowed by *Education Week* on the state, Louisiana's Commissioner of Higher Education, Joseph Savoie, remarked, "This latest recognition by *Education Week* demonstrates yet again that the reform efforts of Louisiana's education community at all levels are appropriately focused and that we're continuing to move in the right direction" (Louisiana Department of Education 2006).

The second set of conditions described above was reported by teachers in the New York City metro area who were interviewed on a wide range of education issues. In a speech on accountability, Joel Klein, chancellor of the New York City public schools said, "Standards mean that we insist on demanding performance criteria for all—not just some—students, and that we make sure that those standards are measurable and demonstrable" (New York City Department of Education 2005). Klein made no mention of school conditions and resources and their relationship to student performance.

A 34-year veteran Wisconsin public school teacher told us, "I will agree to be held accountable for children's test scores when I can be responsible for them 24 hours a day." She was disgusted with the accountability movement's disregard for the societal factors that contribute to poor test performance. We who recently have taught in low-income public schools know that the deck is stacked against poor, mostly minority pupils. We have grown frustrated by the accountability crowd who refuse to admit that hungry, sick, frightened children cannot compete with well-fed, healthy, safe children on test day. The high-stakes testing enthusiasts pretend that all is well with school facilities and at home and that achievement is low because children and their teachers aren't trying hard enough.

In this volume, we argue that closing America's achievement gap cannot be accomplished until the equality gaps in school, at home, and in neighborhoods are addressed and actions are taken to close them. Our research on the differences in children's health care alone has convinced us that corrective justice must be enacted before life-altering decisions continue to be made about students on the basis of high-stakes standardized test scores. Tests qualify as "high stakes" when student performance is used to deny promotion to the next grade, withhold a high school diploma, label schools "failures," determine if teachers and administrators keep their jobs, or decide if schools get more funding. It is the "low performing schools" that get less funding if they are "failures."

We were introduced to the term *corrective justice* in a public law and legal theory working paper by David Lyons (2003), professor of law at Boston University. In our work, we define *corrective justice* as a national commitment to create a level playing field for all public school students who must take the same high-stakes tests. The objectives of corrective justice are affordable housing with reliable running water and electricity; employment opportunities for parents and guardians to make a living wage; top-notch tutors for all children who need them; equity in school buildings, personnel, and resources; adequate medical and dental care for all students; violence-free communities and home lives. These objectives should seem appropriate in a nation where children recite the words, "with liberty and justice for all" before the start of each school day.

The objectives are not utopian. The United States took on an even more formidable effort—the rebuilding of Europe after World War II. On June 5, 1947, Secretary of State George C. Marshall described the rationale and means for such an undertaking. Marshall stated, "Our policy is directed not against any country or doctrine but against hunger, poverty, desperation, and chaos. . . . Political passion and prejudice should have no part" (U.S. Congress 1947). The Marshall Plan required billions of American dollars and know-how.

The Economist (2006), in a discussion of the need for health care reform and other challenges, reports: "These are mightily complicated areas, but the United States has always had a genius for translating the highfalutin' talk of the American Dream into practical policies, such as the GI Bill, a scholarship scheme for returning troops after the second world war. The country needs another burst of practical idealism" (14). Only practical idealism that is fully funded will solve the problems identified in the following pages.

It is hoped that the issues discussed in this book will focus attention on the inherent unfairness of public school accountability mandates and the damage being done to so many by the escalating use of high-stakes testing. In conducting research for this volume, we asked questions of parents, teachers, and public school students in a small sampling of states: California, Colorado, Louisiana, New York, North Carolina, Texas, and Wisconsin. Most of those whose comments we report in these pages reside on Long Island, New York and in New York City. The experiences and insights of these students, parents, and educators clarified the problems that often are overlooked or ignored by state and federal policymakers.

Chapter 1 of this volume presents a history and critique of the high-stakes testing movement in America. In chapter 2, the origins and perpetuation of racism are discussed. Chapter 3 contrasts circumstances of the excluded class with those of the affluent and the ultra rich. Disparities in medical and dental care and their impact on test scores are examined in chapter 4. Neighborhood, school, and home violence and safety concerns are the topics of chapter 5. In chapter 6, differences in school funding and resources are investigated, and in chapter 7, the flourishing tutoring industry is analyzed. Chapter 8 describes

out-of-school, educational enrichment activities enjoyed by children of affluent families—opportunities not available to children of poverty. The after-
word delineates three paths that public education can take in the future. The
path that is chosen depends on America's conscience.

References

Economist. 2006. Inequality and the American dream. June 17–23.

Education Week. 2006. *Quality counts 2006: A decade of standards-based education.*
Bethesda, MD: Education Week.

Lezama, S. 2006. Union schools need clean up to re-open. KNOE-TV (Monroe, LA),
June 14. msnbc.msn.com (accessed June 14, 2006).

Louisiana Department of Education. 2006. Louisiana tops nation in accountability
and teacher quality. www.doe.state.la.us (accessed June 19, 2006).

Lyons, D. 2003. Corrective justice, equal opportunity, and the legacy of slavery and Jim
Crow. Boston University School of Law Working Paper No. 03–15, Public Law and
Legal Theory.

Morrison, I. 2006. State orders Union to fix sick schools. *Monroe (LA) News-Star,* June
8. www.thenewsstar.com (accessed June 8, 2006).

New York City Department of Education. 2005. Speech by Chancellor Joel I. Klein on
newly expanded approach to school accountability. June 7. www.nycenet.edu/
Administration/mediarelations/SpeechesTestimonials (accessed June 20, 2006).

U.S. Congress. *Congressional Record.* 1947. The Marshall Plan. usinfo.state.gov/usa/
infousa/ facts/democrac/57.htm (accessed June 23, 2006).

1

High-Stakes Testing: A Brief History

A FRONT-PAGE EDITORIAL BY SUSAN HERRING (2000) in the *Guardian-Journal*, a weekly Louisiana newspaper, should have alerted state education officials about the toll high-stakes testing could take on a student:

> One fifteen-year-old student felt life was not worth living any more after she failed the LEAP [Louisiana Educational Assessment Program] test in July for the second time. She had been a good student with no behavior or discipline problems, had had problems grasping math problems, but had managed to make a passing grade, then she failed the math portion of the LEAP test. Although she was faithful attending summer remediation courses and said the teachers did a good job, her score in math was lower than her first test score in March. This is the worst case scenario of the pressure exerted upon fourth and eighth graders across the State of Louisiana due to the new high-stakes testing.

Years later, the testing continues unabated.

Origins of High-Stakes Testing

In the 1980s and 1990s the perceived challenge to American corporations by foreign markets led the Business Roundtable (BRT) to begin a campaign to reform public education. The group purported that "to keep up," schools had to return to the basics, meet higher standards, and be held accountable. During the Reagan years, the publication of the booklet, *A Nation at Risk*, by the National Commission on Excellence in Education (1983), served as a lightning rod that demanded public school reform. The report called for "rigorous" standards and attacked "social promotion" policies. It argued that school reform efforts should be guided by experts who understand business and the economy.

The BRT includes the chief executive officers of some of the most well-known corporations in the country, including General Electric, IBM, State Farm Insurance, McGraw-Hill, and General Motors (Business Roundtable 2006). The BRT has set up operations in all 50 states to push for the type of education reform that it believes would be good for the American corporate world. In 1989, the BRT held a summit that led to the reform goals it promoted: outcome-based education, high expectations for all children, strong and complex assessments of student progress, and rewards and punishments for individual schools (Emery and Ohanian 2004, 36–37).

The BRT goals of summer 1989 served as a blueprint for President George H. W. Bush's National Education Goals Summit held in October 1989. In 1995, the BRT pushed a reform strategy that included "Nine Essential Components of a Successful Education System." At the forefront of the nine components were standards, performance assessment, and school accountability. All nine of the essential components were fulfilled federally with the No Child Left Behind (NCLB) Act signed into law by President George W. Bush in 2002.

The BRT also organized the Education Excellence Partnership that included "our nation's leading business, government, and education organizations: the BRT, U.S. Department of Education, Achieve [a promoter of standards-based reform], American Federation of Teachers, National Alliance of Business, National Education Association, National Governors Association, and the U.S. Chamber of Commerce" (newdemocracyworld.org 2002). These groups support standards, accountability, high-stakes testing, and performance consequences. Other high-profile enterprises have supported the testing movement. They include the National Council for Accreditation of Teacher Education (NCATE), an organization that accredits many teacher education institutions, and Educational Testing Service (ETS), a test development organization that has for-profit and not-for-profit divisions.

Sliding, Slippery Language

Michael Apple, John Bascom Professor at the University of Wisconsin, Madison, has illustrated how certain words that have no essential meaning are "mobilized by different groups with different agendas" (Johnson, Johnson, Farenga, and Ness 2005, xii). Apple calls these words *sliding signifiers*. Words such as *democracy, culture,* and *public* fall into this category. Sliding signifiers in education include *accountability, quality, scientific,* and *evidence*. Apple states, "Among the key concepts now sliding around the map of meaning is *standards*" (xii). Although few would oppose the idea of having standards, many questions arise. Johnson et al. (2005, 91) ask

> Where do standards originate? Who sets the standards? What are the standards-setters qualifications? On what basis are standards developed: theoretical assumptions, research findings, some person or group's preferences, political pressures, or some other bases? What special interest groups are at work in the process of standards setting? What convincing research evidence exists that adopting, following and achieving any set of standards leads to improved teaching and learning?

Emery and Ohanian (2004, 6) discuss the language used by the "corporate-politico-media squad." Their depiction of *slippery language* is similar to Apple's sliding signifiers. Included are words and phrases used repeatedly by the BRT and their affiliates until these slippery words take on the meaning that fits their contention: public schools are failing and must be fixed (along their lines). Heard and read enough times, people begin to accept the focused meaning. Among these slippery words and phrases identified by Emery and Ohanian are *credibility and status* (8); *clear, honest, bold data* (9); *highly qualified teacher* (9); *failing schools* (10); *stakeholders* (11); *global marketplace* (12); and *rigorous* or *rigor* (6–7). One encounters these words continuously in the literature of the standards and accountability promoters.

The term *rigor* means severity, strictness, harshness, and rigidity. *Rigor* has nothing to do with excellence, sensibility, goodness, success, challenge, creative thought, or any indicator of a positive quality. But *rigor* is used by the BRT, and affiliated "reformers" such as NCATE, to imply something tough enough to assure quality as in this example: "The NCATE accreditation process establishes rigorous standards for teacher education programs" (NCATE n.d.). Is that what we want in schools and institutions of higher learning—standards and practices that are harsh, strict, exacting, and severe without evidence that these tactics lead to any type of future "success"? In a chapter titled, "The Standards Fraud," Ayers writes, "Standards setting . . . should not be the property of an expert class, the bureaucrats, or special interests. Rather, standard setting should be part of the everyday vocation of schools and communities, the heart and soul of education" (Ayers 2000, 65). Ayers then asks, "What are our standards? I want a teacher in the classroom who is thoughtful and caring, not a mindless clerk or deskilled bureaucrat but a person of substance, depth, and compassion. I want my child to be seen, understood, challenged, and nourished" (68). The standards/accountability/high-stakes testing movement that was launched by the BRT and *A Nation at Risk* has taken public schooling far from the direction Ayers desires.

First in the Nation

Louisiana's state legislature appointed a School Accountability Advising Committee in 1998 (Johnson and Johnson 2002). Its purpose was to establish a system that would hold every child, every teacher, and every school administrator accountable for growth in student achievement as measured by test results. With this legislative mandate, Louisiana, in 2000, became the first state in the nation to base grade promotion on standardized test performance. Fourth- and eighth-grade students who failed to meet predetermined test performance levels were to spend another year in the same grade—based on a single test score. Louisiana was the pioneer state in carrying out the BRT's grand plan. Since 2000, tens of thousands of fourth- and eighth-graders in Louisiana have been flunked and made to spend another year in the same grade. Many of those pupils have been black or poor or both.

The devastation and displacement caused by Hurricane Katrina did not stop the administration of high-stakes tests in some Louisiana school districts less than a year after the hurricane hit. Eighth-graders in one of these districts had two pep rallies prior to the test where "students split into teams, boys on one and girls on the other, to spell the word LEAP (acronym for Louisiana's high-stakes test) across the gym floor with their bodies" (Brumble 2006a). The principal then:

> called students and staff out of the bleachers to jump on a mat and the longer the jump, the more paper money they collected to buy things like game concessions and tickets to dances at school. Everyone wore T-shirts with the theme LEAP for Bucs—as in the school mascot, the buccaneer—that were given to them by the school. The week of testing, all of the school's almost 900 students will get a free snack and juice for breakfast; the employees will have a rib-eye steak at the end of the week in a nod to the so-called high-stakes testing.

An article in the Shreveport, Louisiana, newspaper reported: "It's the season of fear and loathing in fourth grade as students here and across the state prepare for state standardized tests that kick off in two weeks. And with the new iLEAP exam, students as young as seven or eight face their share of pre-testing anxiety this month. Third-, fifth-, sixth-, seventh-, and ninth-graders take iLEAP" (Brumble 2006b).

An elementary school coach said, "There's so much pressure on the kids. I do everything I can to help them with it. And so many fourth-grade teachers feel like if a kid fails the LEAP, they've failed, too."

In Louisiana there is public shaming of school districts and fingerpointing at school personnel if "progress" is deemed unacceptable. A headline in Lafayette's *Daily Advertiser* (2006) states, "Lafayette School District Drops in Rank." The article explains that the district "improved by more than two points on state measurements of school systems, but it wasn't enough as other districts grew faster year over year. The district, ranked 20th in the state last year, dropped to 22 this year—a drop that could have school board members questioning the future of Superintendent James Easton." Another article in a Louisiana newspaper warns, "Bad scores could lead to an overhaul of a school's administration and teaching staff" (Goodnight 2006).

High-stakes test-taking tips abound in local newspapers. The Alexandria, Louisiana daily *Town Talk* (2006) offered the following advice, courtesy of a guidance counselor in the region:

- Make sure that your child has a good night's sleep the night before, and a good breakfast the morning of the test (I've been told that blueberries are "brain" food—but haven't actually seen the research).
- Reduce stress levels in the home by providing a relaxed environment—perhaps by playing classical music, such as Mozart, Bach, or Vivaldi and refraining from arguments.
- Ensure that your child arrives on time and is equipped with the necessary test-taking materials (i.e., #2 pencils, calculator, a healthy snack—if allowed).

Those affected by Hurricane Katrina and the 30 percent of the children living in poverty in Louisiana might have been fresh out of blueberries, Vivaldi concertos, and calculators during test week.

Another problem facing schools in the wake of Louisiana's accountability movement is "overaged" students. Morrison (2006) reports that there is "an ever-increasing population of students far older than their classmates, mostly held back because of policies tied to so-called 'high-stakes' standardized testing, like the LEAP test in fourth and eighth grade." Morrison continues, "Principal Janet Dollar said having a 14-year-old student in a fourth-grade class is not beneficial for that student or his classmates. 'But it's now become evident that there are more overaged kids out there than anticipated,' Dollar said." And critics of public schools wonder why so many students are dropping out.

Recent Developments in High-Stakes Testing

More states have followed Louisiana on this pathway to "public school reform" since 2000. By 2006, there were seven states that made promotion to the next grade in elementary or middle school contingent on performance on a statewide exam: Delaware, Florida, Georgia, Louisiana, Missouri, North Carolina, and Texas (Education Week 2006a, 85). In 23 states, high school graduation is contingent on passing a statewide exit or end-of-course exam. Two additional states are added to this list in 2008 and 2009 (85).

Other accountability policies first envisioned by the BRT are now in place. Florida, Georgia, Illinois, Louisiana, and Tennessee withhold funds from low-performing schools [who need money the most], and 16 states provide rewards to high-performing schools (84). Fourteen states have policies to turn "failing schools" over to private management, 28 states sanction low-performing schools, and ten states allow for the closure of low-performing schools (84–85). All of these consequences are mostly based on scores on high-stakes, standardized tests. There is ever more testing even though research on effective schools has shown that they are effective because they have programs that foster creativity and inquiring minds; they have involved parents, dedicated teachers, and educated support staff. Effective schools are not effective because of high-stakes tests.

Gary Natriello of Columbia University and Aaron Pallas of Michigan State University (*Harvard Gazette* 2000) researched the effects of high-stakes testing on racial groups in Minnesota, New York, and Texas. Their primary finding is that majority group students outperformed minority students in all cases. They found that test-prep drills might raise pass rates by a few points, but most students are unable to use those skills in other reading tasks. The researchers write, "What we are finding out . . . is truly frightening: when high-stakes tests drive education reform, they can reduce the curriculum in high-poverty schools to little more than test preparation." Such tests ignore the research on the importance of helping children develop cumulative skills and understandings that can be transferred to other materials and situations. The "learning" of discrete, brief bits of information is information that soon is forgotten.

Linda McNeil of Rice University and Angela Valenzuela of the University of Texas conducted research on the impact of high-stakes testing in Texas (*Harvard Gazette* 2000). They conclude that the high-stakes Texas test "masks the real problems of inequity that underlie the failure to adequately educate children. By shifting funds, public attention and scarce organizational and budgetary resources away from schools and into the coffers of the testing industry vendors, the futures of poor and minority children and the schools they attend get compromised."

The findings of these researchers affirm common sense. The studies contribute to the mounting evidence that local-, state-, and federally mandated high-stakes testing is doing more harm than good. One reason why children of the excluded class perform below children of the middle and upper classes on high-stakes tests is the lack of linguistic stimulation in most impoverished environments. Kirp (2006) reports on a study conducted by Hart and Risley: "By the time they are four years old, children growing up in poor families have typically heard a total of 32 million fewer spoken words than those whose parents are professionals. That language gap translates directly into stunted academic trajectories" (16).

Standards, high-stakes testing, and accountability fly in the face of everything we know about human learning. Callahan (2005, 775) notes:

> While there are obvious physical differences among children and adults (height, weight, manual dexterity, speed, agility, etc.), the focus on individual differences in the classroom is generally in the realm of cognitive differences and sometimes crosses over into behavioral domains that may impair the learning process. The cognitive differences that have been measured and used in decisionmaking in classrooms range from global concepts, such as general intellectual ability (IQ), to very specific differences in learning styles and interests.

Thus, each person is a unique individual with a different level of intelligence, different prior knowledge and experiences, different interests, different types of creativity, and different health conditions. Individuals come from different family sizes and compositions, different community types, and different peer groups. They come from different levels of family income.

Until the mid-1980s, American teachers were recognized as the experts that they are. Teachers were viewed as the ones who knew the subject matter, knew their students, and knew the community. They understood that good teaching meant taking every child or youth as he or she walks through the classroom door and helping each of them advance as far as possible—knowing that the next year's teacher would do the same. Students were not expected to be on the same "level" on anything. That is not the nature of the human condition.

In the past two decades, since standards, accountability, and high-stakes testing have become dominant in public schooling, all of that has changed. Teachers have lost much of their autonomy, and their wisdom and expertise often are ignored. Corporate executives, politicians, and bureaucrats now make the major education decisions. Such individuals and groups dictate what will be taught at each grade, how it will be taught, how long it will be taught, how learning will be assessed, what constitutes success and failure, and what the consequences will be for failure. The joy of learning and teaching has been squeezed out of many public school classrooms by the pressures to prepare for the tests to nudge the scores a few points higher so that some politicians can boast of the success of their "reform" effort. The stresses caused by high-stakes testing and the inherent unfairness of the testing-as-reform mentality have led to an escalating barrage of criticisms of such policies.

Criticisms of High-Stakes Testing

Critics of high-stakes testing have included parents, classroom teachers, researchers, scholars, professional organizations, and concerned citizens. One such critic is Yale psychologist Robert Sternberg (2002) who summarized negative factors related to testing.

Sternberg writes that tests and testing procedures are flawed and standardized test scores are unreliable. The major professional research and testing organizations including the American Educational Research Association (AERA), the American Psychological Association (APA), and the National Council on Measurement in Education (NCME) have documented the likelihood of error within the standardized tests and their administration and scoring. As Sternberg points out, "The use of standardized tests as the sole measure of whether students are promoted, are placed in low-track classes, or will graduate from high school is condemned as insupportable by every testing organization in the country" (2).

Flaws in test scoring have created serious problems for numbers of students and have caused the retraction of test results in some states. When two-thirds of tenth-graders failed the statewide math Regents exams in 2003, New York created a new scoring system that enabled most of those students to pass (Johnson and Johnson 2006, 203). In Georgia, statewide testing for 600,000 fifth-graders was cancelled because of testing errors. Test errors also have been reported in Massachusetts, Nevada, Louisiana, and elsewhere (203–205). *Education Week* (2006b) reports that 355 Connecticut high school students were given incorrect state accountability test scores by Harcourt Assessment Inc. *Education Week* notes that the revised scores "will force local officials to re-evaluate whether those students will be eligible to graduate." The Connecticut Commissioner of Education predicted that mistakes by testing companies would escalate and said, "I continue to question whether testing every student every year in every state in seven grades is simply too overwhelming" (18).

In an open letter to New York City Schools Chancellor Joel Klein, Jane Hirschman (2004), president of Time Out from Testing, writes:

> The test [3rd grade high-stakes test] reflects a bias toward white children . . . 11 questions favor white children; 0 favor Hispanic children . . . 0 favor African American children.

The technical report presents no evidence on how passing scores on the test have been set. . . . The error of measurement on the ELA [English Language Arts] test could lead to a swing of plus or minus 10,000 children failing the test and being "flunked" to repeat grade three.

In early 2006, 225,000 New York State seventh-graders took a statewide English test that had a flawed answer sheet. Herszenhorn (2006, B1) reports, "The exam booklet directed students to choose F, G, H, or J as possible answers while the answer sheet offered only A, B, C, D as options." On other questions, the reverse was the case. Teachers were directed to use the chalkboard to show pupils how to use the A B C D bubbles to mark F G H J answers and the reverse. State officials maintained that the CTB/McGraw-Hill tests still were valid despite this flaw. Parents expressed concern that the mistake caused additional stress for children already filled with test anxiety. One parent stated, "My daughter was hysterical. She was convinced she messed up and she was going to be held over" (B8).

In March 2006, the College Board announced that there were errors in scoring the SAT test taken in October by those students applying for college admission and financial aid. Arenson (2006c, 18) writes that the College Board "notified colleges of corrections for 4,411 students whose scores were too low—by as many as 450 points out of a possible 2,400—but is not making changes for 600 other students whose scores were too high." Acceptance decisions already had been made for many students when the scoring errors were revealed. Walters and Farrell (2006, A45) report:

Pearson [Pearson Educational Measurement] has issued a news release stating that part of the reason for the error was "abnormally high moisture content" in some of the answer sheets. This moisture caused the answer-sheet paper to expand, leading to inaccurate renditions of students' answers during the scanning process. Every testing center in the United States sends the answer sheets via overnight mail to Pearson's scanning warehouse in Austin, Tex. On the test day, torrential rain fell in some parts of the Northeast.

Now college admission and scholarship decisions can hinge on the weather?

A college dean of admissions said, "A swing of even 80 or 100 points on the SAT could mean the difference between the highest-level scholarship or not receiving one at all, because it is so competitive" (Arenson 2006c, 18).

Shortly after the SAT scoring errors were disclosed, there was an $11 million settlement from ETS (Educational Testing Service) for scoring errors on a teacher certification exam. The case involved 27,000 test takers. Late test delivery, test misprints, collating errors, and sample test items repeated on the actual tests were reported in Illinois and New York. These are some of the publicized problems with standardized tests. W. James Popham, UCLA emeritus professor, said, "Frankly, because it is in the best public-relations interest of both the scoring service and the state officials who hire them, many scoring muck-ups are masked" (Arenson 2006b, A13).

Sternberg (2002) argues that test scores only are meaningful in the entire contexts of the children. What opportunities have the children had to learn? Have the families and the school been able to provide resources essential for learning? Are the schools overcrowded? Are the teachers well-trained and certified? Test scores show a strong correlation with a child's family education level, financial well-being, and home environment. It is well-known that a high-stakes test score is more closely related to family income than to anything that has occurred in school test preparation.

Stephanie Galde, a New York academic intervention service provider said in an interview,

> On the final day of the fourth-grade ELA (English Language Arts high-stakes test), a student didn't have number 2 pencils with him and he hadn't eaten breakfast—he had forgotten that there was one more day of the test. This poor 10-year-old had been stressed out enough for two days and now he had hit his breaking point. He was hysterically crying. Is this the message New York State is trying to send to its children? Go to school, fail some tests, and don't move on to the next grade? Growing up, I always viewed school as a safe place—somewhere to go that would protect me—and here I have this child crying hysterically in my classroom because of a test.

High-stakes testing can be harmful to children's health. The pressures and anxiety associated with the constant drumbeat of testing, testing, and more testing are making children more than "hysterical"—they are making children sick. Johnson and Johnson (2006, 131–132), as teachers in a high-poverty, mostly black elementary school in Louisiana, observed weeks before the testing: "The children are exhausted from all of the skill-and-drill overkill of the past weeks. They are not their usual ebullient selves. They are jittery and smile infrequently. There are more arguments and more physical confrontations among pupils. Students and teachers alike are showing the signs of stress." During the testing, one of the teachers in the school recalled: "I pass out the coded answer folders and read from the script in the administrator's booklet. As the children begin the first timed test, Kelvin vomits in his hands and runs to the bathroom. He does not complete the first section. I must document this. Gerard takes one look at the first section and begins to cry. He picks up his pencil and, between sobs, randomly fills in bubbles on the answer folder" (132–133).

One of our graduate students, Barry Wilson, who is a father of a fourth-grader in a New York public school, sent us the following e-mail:

My son is about to take the fourth-grade ELA exams this week. He has experienced extreme anxiety, vomiting, diarrhea, and has been unable to sleep in his own bed for the last three days. It's breaking my heart. He wants to do so well. A nine-year-old should not be subjected to this. No Child Left Behind is not a remedy, it's a horror for our children. How can I help to ensure that other children are not subjected to this kind of gross anxiety?

Emery and Ohanian (2004, 186) write: "Every child's so-called reading ability is tested and reported out with a precision that infects every moment in school. Instead of nurturing children for who they are and for what they can do, instead of fostering a joy in reading, schools now make kids afraid they aren't good enough; they make kids vomit. How did we get to this point where parents send their children off to a place that makes them vomit?"

Every teacher in a high-stakes test environment is aware of the headaches, stomachaches, and other symptoms exhibited by children but also by teachers and principals. One can feel the fear in the air at test time—fear of failure with grim consequences for all involved. Children's book authors even have documented this fear in works such as *Testing Miss Malarkey* (Finchler 2000). Barbara Mendez, one of our California interviewees, commented: "It saddens me that children are the ones to bear the brunt of all this political propaganda and these financial schemes. How can anyone refer to standards and high-stakes testing as *educational reform* when it has such profound negative effects on children's emotional and physical well-being?"

Sternberg (2002, 4) contends that high-stakes testing is causing more students to drop out of school and more good teachers to flee the profession. In a confirmation of this assertion, Sentell (2005) reports on an alarming increase in public school dropouts in Louisiana in recent years. The increase in dropouts has been documented in the popular news media as well as in education newspapers. *USA Today* (2006) lists fourteen large urban school districts where fewer than 50 percent of the students graduate from high school. In Detroit the graduation rate is 21.7 percent, in Baltimore it is 38.5 percent, and in New York City it is 38.9 percent. *Education Week* (2006c) lists graduation rates by race and ethnicity, among other factors, for large school districts and for states. Graduation rates range from 47.4 percent of American Indian high schoolers to 51.6 percent of African American highschoolers to 77 percent of Asian high schoolers. Seventy-six percent of white high schoolers graduate. Overall, the highest percentage of high school graduates (78.6 percent) occurs in school districts with low poverty; there is a 60 percent graduation rate in school districts with high poverty. The pressures of high-stakes testing and awareness of impending failure have contributed to the dropout crisis.

This is not promising news for our country and should shake up the BRT who need skilled workers to keep their corporations afloat. It should alert them that the standards/accountability movement that they have promoted is not working and the problem is more complex than administering high-stakes tests. In addition to the dropouts, there are the pushouts. These are the students who are pushed out of their school because they will not make the school look good when accountability scores are computed. Medina and Lewin (2003) reported on high schools who try to dump students who might negatively affect a school's score. One of the schools featured had a poverty rate of 90 percent among the student body. Medina and Lewin state:

> Those who run adult-education programs and alternative high schools say that as a result of the increasing pressure for schools to show better graduation rates, more and more students, and ever-younger ones, are being pushed out of their regular high schools as soon as they fall behind. . . . Experts say the pressure to produce good results inevitably forces principals to find ways to unload students who may not graduate on time. (B6)

High-stakes testing also is chipping away at our teaching force. Sternberg (2002, 5) cites a Texas State Reading Association survey which found that 85 percent of the respondents agreed with the statement: "The emphasis on TAAS [the mandatory Texas test now called TAKS] is forcing some of the best teachers to leave teaching." According to our interviewees, the same thing is happening in other states. Beverly McDaniels, a veteran Wisconsin teacher, is taking early retirement because of overtesting. Lisa Zanders, a former Colorado middle school teacher, left the classroom for the business world because of the "overemphasis on standards and testing."

In an unpublished study titled, "Where Do Louisiana Principals Stand?" (personal communication 2004) a survey of Louisiana school principals showed that 74 percent of the principals believed that high-stakes testing and accountability are driving teachers out of the classroom. In the same survey, 88 percent of the principals thought that state legislators (who mandated the testing) do not have sound knowledge of standardized testing or the extraneous variables such as hunger, poor health, and community violence that can affect test scores.

Sternberg (2002, 5) claims: "Standardization is the enemy of effective public schools. . . . Pressure to raise test scores above all other educational goals has the effect of impoverishing the curriculum. Schools across the country have already eliminated advanced electives, music and art classes, science classes, physical education, and study of current events in part because these subjects do not appear on high-stakes standardized tests." Sternberg quotes Michael McGill, superintendent of schools in Scarsdale, New York, who decried the inflexible education that has been the result of the standards movement: "They've diverted attention from important local goals, highlighted simplistic and sometimes inappropriate tests, needlessly promoted similarity in curriculum and teaching. To the extent they've caused education to regress to a state average, they've undermined excellence" (6).

Dillon (2006) reports that according to a nationwide survey conducted by the Center on Education Policy, 71 percent of America's schools have pared their curricula to spend more time on reading and math—the two subjects that have been the emphasis of NCLB. One school in California identified by Dillon, Martin Luther King Jr. Junior High School, allows its lowest scoring students to take only reading, math, and physical education—hardly a well-rounded curriculum. It should be no surprise that 89 percent of the school's pupils are on free or reduced lunch. The state average is 50 percent on free or reduced lunch (greatschools.net 2006).

Sylvia Lopez, a parent of school-aged children in New York, told us:

> During test week, my children cannot fall asleep at night, wake up hours early in the morning, and are crabby, nervous, and angry. They fight with each other and my home becomes a battleground. They are overburdened with reading comprehension or math problems, packet after packet. My eight-year-old daughter told me the week after the English test in January they were going to start doing math all day, several days of the week, until the state math assessment in March.

In a Gallup/Phi Delta Kappa poll (Rose and Gallup 2005, 50) of the public's attitudes toward the public schools, 82 percent of the respondents were concerned a great deal or a fair amount that high-stakes testing in English and math means less emphasis on art, music, history, and other subjects. If only this 82 percent would make their views known to their local, state, and national elected officials.

High-stakes test results most strongly reflect neighborhood and family socioeconomic status—not student learning. The tests punish poor, minority, special needs, and non-English-speaking students who must compete with children of affluence on the same tests. Decades of research on the importance of prior knowledge and experience on reading comprehension [including test passage comprehension] have shown that those who lack sufficient prior knowledge are at a major disadvantage (Johnson and Johnson 2006, 210).

In our interviews with students, the importance of prior knowledge became apparent. None of our middle school interviewees who came from affluent families on Long Island could define *food stamps* accurately. One student said, "Stamps with pictures of food." Another said, "To tell what the food is in the package," and a third said, "Aren't they the little stickers they put on apples and bananas?" These same children, however, accurately defined *orthodontist*, *passport,* and *boarding pass.* The students from low-socioeconomic status (SES) families, who were the same ages as the affluent students, invariably defined *food stamps* accurately (e.g., "a form of coupon money for people in poverty," "fake money used by poor people but only to buy food"). One child couldn't define the word but said, "My mother pays for food with them." None of the economically poor knew the meanings of *orthodontist, passport,* or *boarding pass.*

Peggy Reginald, a first grade teacher, told us:

> I often think of an incident that occurred while giving E-Class exams which are given to the children in New York City individually by the teacher at the beginning and end of each year. The children had to read a story called, "I Love Mess" and then answer a series of questions. The story was about a girl who liked to make a mess, but it made her parents mad. She could make her parents happy by cleaning up. One of the questions asked, "Why is it a good idea to keep your room clean?" The "correct" answers were "to make your parents happy" or "to know where our things are." Eighteen out of my 22 students answered that they need to keep their room clean so that they don't get bugs. They used their background knowledge—messes mean bugs.

Poor children who have traveled little; who have few books or other resources at home; whose minimum-wage, single parents may have little time for language interaction with them; are at a testing disadvantage. Test passage comprehension has more to do with prior knowledge and experience than with test preparation drills.

Criticisms of No Child Left Behind

Public Law 107–110, called the No Child Left Behind (NCLB) Act, was passed by Congress in 2001 and signed into law by President George W. Bush on January 8, 2002. With this new act, high-stakes testing became the law of the land. It mandated that every public school child in grades three through eight must be tested every year in reading and math. The law further required that every public school child must be "proficient" in reading and math by 2014 [a pedagogical impossibility]. The new law established a federal accountability system that linked standardized testing to heavy sanctions for schools that failed to make "adequate yearly progress" (AYP). Each year, test scores were to inch higher for every subgroup of students as determined by race, family income, disability, and native language.

Other provisions of NCLB included a demand for "highly qualified" teachers, a sliding signifier that has taken on many definitions, including simply passing a test for teachers without having had any academic teacher preparation. The law also permits the transfer of students out of any public school that fails to meet adequate yearly progress.

NCLB has empowered the federal government to add to the testing pressures that some states and school districts already had placed on children, particularly children of low-income families. At the same time that public school-children are overtested, made to endure continuous test preparation instead of real educational experiences, and made to suffer the indignities and emotional pain of having to repeat a grade in school because they failed a single test, most private schoolchildren are free to learn, and their teachers are free to teach. Unless things change, we foresee the growth of an educated elite with every advantage, and a test-weary, lockstep-thinking majority who attend the public schools.

In 2004, civil rights, education, child advocacy, and citizens' organizations issued a joint statement that expressed their concerns with NCLB. Among the 31 organizations were the National School Boards Association, the American Association of School Administrators, the Children's Defense Fund, and the American Association of University Women. The statement says, in part:

> Among these concerns are: overemphasizing standardized testing; narrowing curriculum and instruction to focus on test preparation rather than richer academic learning; over-identifying schools in need of improvement; using sanctions that do not help improve schools; inappropriately excluding low-scoring children in order to boost test results; and inadequate funding. (FairTest 2004)

Other opponents of NCLB include emerita Stanford professor Nell Noddings; Deborah Meier, New York University professor; Gerald W. Bracey, education researcher and columnist for *Phi Delta Kappan*; and Mary Sorrells, classroom teacher in Ashville, North Carolina. Noddings (2005, 38), in "Rethinking a Bad Law," discussed the effects of NCLB on the morale of students, teachers, and administrators. She decries the narrowing of the curriculum that has been the result of high-stakes testing and NCLB:

> If the No Child Left Behind legislation was designed to provide better schooling, especially for poor and minority students, the result is deeply troubling. For it is the curriculum of these children that seems to have been gutted. Wealthier kids, in schools that don't have to worry so much about test scores, may still enjoy arts, music, drama, projects, and critical conversation. But poor kids are spending far too much time bent over worksheets and test prep materials.

Noddings offers sound recommendations such as fixing rundown schools, providing dental and vision services for pupils, and providing homeless children places to stay—things the authors of this volume refer to as *corrective justice*. It appears, however, that all of the money is going to the testing and none to the real needs of children. Bracey (2005) pointed out the absurdity of punishing entire schools with "failing" labels when only one group of students (e.g., special needs children) or another fails to make adequate yearly progress. Meier (2004), in an article titled, "No Politician Left Behind," claims that NCLB is built on an illusion that tests alone can ensure school reform, that penalties motivate teachers and children, and that "inadequate resources" is simply an excuse. She writes that nearly all individuals closest to the action, including teachers, principals, and school boards, oppose the law—but they oppose it quietly and fearfully.

Not all teachers, however, have remained fearful and quiet. Sorrells (2002, 52), in a letter to *Education Week*, referred to high-stakes testing as "high-threat testing." She observes:

> Threatening all of our students, teachers, and principals every year with dire consequences based on test results is a horrendous practice. Children are threatened with retention. Teachers are threatened with less pay, and everyone is threatened with publication of the results. . . . Decisions on retention should be made using multiple assessment tools by the people who know each student. And a school should not be labeled a "school of distinction" or "exemplary" or anything else based on standardized test results.

The Finland Model

Perhaps the United States could take some lessons from Finland if our goal is to elevate test scores so we can compete globally as the BRT wants. Finland ranks first among 29 industrialized nations on the Program for International Assessment in mathematical literacy and problem solving (Cavanagh 2005). It ranks number one on other international comparisons of reading and literacy skills and science. Finland has lower percentages of low-performing students than other nations, and a smaller gap between the highest and lowest test scores than most countries, including the United States (8). What is Finland's education system being allowed to do that contributes to these top international ratings?

Among the characteristics of Finland's school system, teachers, and students identified by Cavanagh are the following:

1. Cities, schools, and teachers have considerable autonomy in determining course content, choosing their textbooks, and planning the instruction.

Teachers and schools have much more responsibility for what is taught and how it is taught than is true in the United States in the present era.

2. Schools in Finland use standardized tests, too, but they are used to provide information to the schools about student performance. In Finland there are no penalties for student or school performances on tests.

3. Classes in Finland are organized heterogeneously. That is, classes are comprised of stronger and weaker students.

4. In recognition of the greater difficulty of teaching students of a wide range of abilities in the same class, class sizes in Finland are kept small.

5. Finland's students use the library more and display the highest interest in reading of any of the 29 industrialized nations in the study.

6. All teachers in Finland must hold a Master's degree. Teachers in Finland are respected, and teaching is a prestigious profession. Entry into teacher preparation programs is highly competitive and only one applicant in nine is admitted.

Finnish schools, like many European and Japanese schools, are organized into 45-minute class periods followed by a 15-minute break for teachers and students. This is in contrast to the increasing practice in American public schools of eliminating recess periods to free up more time for test preparation. Research conducted by Pellegrini and Bohn (2005) demonstrated through experimental and longitudinal data the importance of recess breaks in maximizing children's cognitive performance. Benefits of recess periods include improved school learning, improved pupil physical health, and stronger social competence brought about by the recess opportunities to interact with peers (13–19).

In comparison with Finland, many American public schools, under the pressures of standards, accountability, and high-stakes testing, seem to be doing all of the wrong things and none of the right ones. If we followed Finland's lead and returned curricular and instructional autonomy and authority to teachers and schools, removed punitive consequences for test failure, and restored respect for teachers, we would be moving in the right direction.

Finland is a much smaller country (roughly three times the size of Ohio) and a much less populous nation (about 5 million people in 2003) than the United States. Ninety-three percent of the population is ethnic Finn, and 90 percent of Finns share the same religion, so racism and discrimination are not a major concern. Finland is the least corrupt country in the world, according to the Berlin-based Transparency International Corruption Perceptions Index. The United States ranks sixteenth. Finland ranks in the top ten countries with the greatest equality of income between the poorest and the richest citizens. The United States is not among the top ten (*Time Almanac 2004*, 2003, 713, 714, 774–775). The *Economist* (2006) states that in the United States, "The gap between the rich and poor is bigger than in any other advanced country" (28), and "only 3 percent of students at top colleges come from the poorest quarter of the population. Poor children are trapped in dismal schools, while richer parents spend ever more cash on tutoring their offspring" (13). Although the United States cannot replicate Finland's small size or its homogeneous composition, we can strive for greater equity of income and resources—factors essential for corrective justice.

Testing Preschool Children

The obsession with high-stakes testing and accountability engineered by the BRT through compliant and willing state legislatures and departments of education has now spread to kindergarten, preschool, and Head Start programs. High-stakes testing in these early years is now rampant and the notion of a "developmentally appropriate curriculum" has been replaced by the imposition of rigid standards. Jacobson (2004) reported that 36 states now have standards specifying what four-year-olds should know and be able to do before entering kindergarten. The number of preschool standards varies from state to state and ranges from 50 to 370 different standards. Those who have worked with very young children know that many of them come to school not knowing how to take turns, how to modulate their voices, or other group interaction skills. The transformation from a focus on social skills to an academic focus ignores a century of research on early childhood education. Standards for reading, writing, and math in preschool place unwarranted stress on the very young, disregard the importance of play in learning, and rob young children of essential parts of their childhoods.

President George W. Bush pushed for the overhaul of Head Start, the federally funded preschool program for economically disadvantaged children. Bush's goal was to transform the emphasis from health, nutrition, and social skills to academics. The testing program he put in place for Head Start assesses letter recognition, vocabulary, and early mathematics skills. The President stated, "We want excellence . . . we want Head Start to set higher ambitions for the millions of children it serves" (Bumiller 2003, A1, A18).

Many questions on the Head Start test are "class-biased and inappropriate," according to Bruno (2004). Vocabulary questions include having children look at sketchy black-and-white drawings and then asking them to point to the picture of a *swamp*. Another question calls for identifying *vase* from pictures of a decanter, a canister, a trophy, and a vase. A third question requires that children look at sketches of four different facial expressions and identify which one is *horrified*. How many four-year-olds know the words *swamp* or *horrified*, and why should they? How many four-year-olds can discern the difference between a vase, a decanter, and a canister, and again, why should they? The test has 24 such items. Who chose these words and test formats? It could not have been someone with much experience with four-year-olds.

The National Association for the Education of Young Children (NAEYC) has condemned the Head Start test that is called the National Reporting System (NRS). Meisels and Atkins-Burnett (2004) report:

> The NRS is biased toward children from families with high socioeconomic status and Caucasian culture. Not only is it class- and race-oriented, it also reflects a singular pedagogical approach. It has few expressive and no creative, constructive, or active elements. . . . The lessons it teaches Head Start staff are negative regarding children's potential, and it does not recognize the richness of the backgrounds that Head Start children bring with them.
>
> This test is not good early education practice. It is not good psychometric practice. It is not good public policy. And it is certainly not good for young children.

Borja (2005) reported on the increase in preschool tutoring programs offered by such for-profit, test-prep giants as Sylvan Learning Centers, Kumon North America, Score! Educational Centers, Inc. (a subsidiary of Kaplan Learning), and Headsprout, Inc. The emphasis on academic standards, high-stakes testing, and accountability in the preschool has led to a new phenomenon in American education: expelling three- and four-year-olds from school. A study released by the Yale Child Study Center in 2005 found that "preschool children are three times as likely to be expelled as children in primary school, and that roughly 5,000 preschool children are turned out each year" (Steinhauer 2005, 1, 4). Preschoolers, normally egocentric, need to learn to share, need to learn to lose without throwing a tantrum, and need to engage in interactive play. The requirement to identify beginning sounds of words, count to a preestablished number, and engage in rote tasks can be monotonous and can stifle enthusiasm for school. A number of preschoolers cannot handle the regimentation, so they exhibit behavioral problems and get expelled from preschool for being "unready to learn" or "hard to control." They are the victims of inappropriate expectations brought about by political insistence on ever-higher levels of achievement as determined by high-stakes tests.

Yet Another Test

Saulny (2005) reports that under intense pressure from the Business Council of New York State, an affiliate of the BRT, the Board of Regents and the Department of Education are developing a "work readiness" credential. New York already requires that public school students pass five Regents exams to graduate from high school. Saulny notes, "But business leaders have been clear that the current system is not measuring up" (2). The work readiness credential would require that students pass a test that would evaluate skills in 10 areas, including following directions, communicating, making decisions, and speaking skills. The test would enable employers to make hiring decisions.

Richard P. Mills, the Commissioner of Education in New York, has, during his 10 years in office, made New York public school students among the most tested in America. He is a member of the Workplace Investment Board, a main proponent of the new work readiness credential. Mills stated, "We must redouble our efforts to guarantee to students, parents, and the employer community that the diploma means ready to work" (Saulny 2005, 2).

New York and Louisiana are the two states that annually seem to vie for first or second place for their public school accountability programs. For 10 years, *Education Week* has published an annual report card on which each state is awarded a grade, *A* through *F*, on several factors. Among the factors are standards and accountability, school climate, resource equity, and efforts to improve teacher quality. *Education Week* analyzes each state's standardized testing program, their report cards for public schools, and their sanctions or rewards for low- or high-performing schools to determine standards and accountability grades.

Strict accountability mandates, however, as measured by *Education Week*, do not translate into educational excellence. Some states (e.g., Iowa, Maine, Minnesota, Nebraska, New Hampshire, Rhode Island, and Wyoming) that receive the lowest accountability grades from *Education Week*, grades of *C*, *D*, or *F*, have public education systems of recognized excellence. States that were awarded an *A* from *Education Week* include Florida, Georgia, Indiana, Louisiana, New York, Ohio, and South Carolina (*Education Week* 2006, 80). Some of these are states that one typically does not associate with educational excellence. Perhaps with its new workplace credential and the accompanying standards and standardized test, New York will recapture the "first place in accountability" crown from the current number one, Louisiana.

High-Stakes Testing in Higher Education

In late 2005, President George W. Bush established the Commission on the Future of Higher Education. Charles Miller, a private investor and former chairman of the University of Texas Board of Regents, was named chair of the

Commission. He immediately introduced the idea of federal implementation of standardized testing in the nation's colleges and universities for the purposes of accountability and standards setting. Miller wrote a memorandum to the 18 other Commission members in which he stated, "What is clearly lacking is a nationwide system for comparative performance purposes, using standard formats" (Arenson 2006a). When Miller headed the University of Texas Regents, all nine campuses were directed to give standardized tests "to prove students were learning." U.S. Secretary of Education Margaret Spellings (2005) announced, "It is time to examine how we can get the most out of our national investment in higher education. We have a responsibility to make sure our higher education system continues to meet our nation's needs for an educated and competitive workforce in the 21st century."

If Mr. Miller's recommendation to the Commission becomes national policy, our federal government will have in place the mandates for high-stakes testing in public schools from Head Start and preschool to graduate school. This would be a stunning accomplishment for the BRT. In just 20 years, the nation's public education system will have been transformed to a test-driven, teach-for-the-test educational enterprise at all levels.

David L. Warren, president of the National Association of Independent Colleges and Universities, registered his disapproval of the Commission's high-stakes testing ambitions. Warren states, "What we oppose is a single, national, high-stakes, one-size-fits-all, über-outcome exam. The notion of a single exam implies there are national standards, and that implies a national curriculum. Then we are on the way to a centralized Prussian education system" (Arenson 2006a). One member of the Commission on the Future of Higher Education perhaps will be supportive of the testing and accountability plan set forth by Chairman Miller. That person is Jonathan Grayer, chairman and CEO of Kaplan, Inc., one of the largest testing and tutoring corporations in the nation.

The Transfer of Learning

There is no evidence that standards and accountability equate to the quality of the education experience, how engaged students are in their learning, or how well they are learning. There is ample evidence that what is measured on state high-stakes tests does not transfer to other situations. Transfer of learning undergirds the major function of schooling. If learning does not transfer, then nearly everything anyone encounters must be learned from scratch. Bigge (1982, 253) notes:

> The effectiveness of a school depends, in a large measure, upon the amount and quality of transfer potential of the materials that students learn. Thus, transfer of learning is the cornerstone upon which education should ultimately rest. Unless

students learn in school those matters that help them in meeting situations more effectively further along the academic sequence and later in life as well as in the present, they are wasting much of their time.

Amrein and Berliner (2002) analyzed testing data from 18 states that have severe consequences attached to their high-stakes tests. They were looking for any signs that these testing programs had an effect on learning as measured by four nationally recognized standardized achievement tests: National Assessment of Educational Progress (NAEP), Advanced Placement (AP), Scholastic Aptitude Test (SAT), and American College Testing Program (ACT). The researchers wanted to determine if there was any transfer from the state tests to these established, widely recognized measures. Amrein and Berliner conclude, "Evidence from this study of 18 states with high-stakes tests is that in all but one analysis, student learning [on any of the four recognized tests] is indeterminate, remains at the same level as it was before the policy was implemented, or actually goes down when high-stakes testing policies are instituted" (2).

Who will be held accountable for the lack of transfer of learning from test to test or to authentic, everyday reading tasks? The BRT and its associates, state legislators, state superintendents of education, state boards and departments of education, the Bush administration and the Congress that enacted NCLB must all be held accountable. Billions of dollars continue to be wasted on all the offshoots of accountability mandates. The taxpayers, teachers, and especially the test takers deserve some answers.

Testing and the Corporate Bottom Line

State and federal mandated testing has led to a financial bonanza for corporations in the testing, publishing, and tutoring industries. According to Olson (2004), the federal Government Accountability Office has estimated that testing requirements will cause states to spend more than $5 billion in the next few years. Nine companies, including CTB/McGraw-Hill, Harcourt Assessment, Pearson Assessments, and Riverside Publishing, have garnered 87 percent of the testing business. Giant tutoring corporations such as Sylvan Learning, Kaplan K–12, the Princeton Review, Huntington Learning Centers, Inc., Plato Learning, Inc., and some smaller firms are cashing in on the $2 billion tutoring market (see chapter 7). Large and small publishers of school books, computer software, and other test preparation materials are having a field day. Nearly every public school in the nation facing high-stakes tests feels compelled to buy any kind of test-preparation materials to elevate their test scores. This especially is true of struggling schools, inner-city and rural, that serve students of poverty, minorities, and students learning English as a second language. These schools face nasty consequences if high-stakes test scores do not climb: public embarrassment and shame brought on by public display of test scores; school sanctions, including reconstitution or closure; and loss of tax revenues because of student transfers as encouraged by NCLB.

No state or the federal government needs any test data to determine which schools require the most help. They are the schools (often resegregated) that serve primarily African Americans, Hispanics, and other minorities. They are the schools that serve the millions of children who live in poverty in this rich nation. They are the schools that are deprived of adequate up-to-date teaching materials and resources. They are the schools of rat- and roach-infested crumbling buildings with inadequate heat, no hot water, and iffy electrical wiring. Gaetano Caputo, a teacher in the New York City public schools said,

> Many an afternoon I have to spend time turning my chalkboard into a makeshift screen by using white bulletin board paper. I'm sure the New York City Board of Education has given millions of dollars to organizations, universities and so-called specialists to try to rectify the problem of poor standardized test scores. If only that money had been used to supply the classroom teachers with materials necessary to teach such as paper, writing supplies, computer software, overhead projectors, and screens.

Wouldn't it make sense to discontinue all the high-stakes testing and other accountability mandates and dismantle the accountability fiefdoms at all levels of government? Then all those billions of dollars that would be saved could be channeled to the schools that need the support that money can buy.

In the following chapter, we examine chronic racism that makes everyday living in our country a struggle for its victims.

References

Alexandria (LA) Town Talk. 2006. High-stakes testing tips. March 11. www.thetown talk.com (accessed March 11, 2006).

Amrein, A. L., and D. C. Berliner. 2002. High-stakes testing, uncertainty, and student learning. *Education Policy Analysis Archives* 10 (18): 1–69.

Arenson, K. W. 2006a. Panel explores standard tests for colleges. *New York Times*, February 9. www.newyorktimes.com/2006/02/09/education/09testing.html (accessed February 14, 2006).

———. 2006b. Testing errors prompt calls for oversight. *New York Times*, March 18, A1, A13.

———. 2006c. Colleges say SAT mistakes may affect scholarships. *New York Times*, March 26, 18.

Ayers, W. 2000. The standards fraud. In *Will standards save public education?* ed. D. Meier, 64–69. Boston: Beacon Press.

Bigge, M. L. 1982. *Learning theories for teachers.* 4th ed. New York: Harper and Row.

Borja, R. R. 2005. Growing niche for tutoring chains: Prekindergartners' academic prep. *Education Week,* October 19, 10.

Bracey, G. 2005. The seven deadly absurdities of No Child Left Behind. EdNews.org. www.educationnews.org/seven-deadly-absurdities.htm (accessed October 10, 2005).

Brumble, M. 2006a. High-stakes testing to go on as usual in northwest Louisiana. *Shreveport (LA) Times,* March 12. www.shreveporttimes.com (accessed March 12, 2006).

———. 2006b. Visualization, breathing, exercise help reduce pre-test stress. *Shreveport (LA) Times,* March 17. www.shreveporttimes.com (accessed March 17, 2006).

Bruno, L. 2004. Preschoolers get head start on tough testing. *Morris County (NJ) Daily Record News,* March 14. www.dailyrecord.com/news/articles/news1-headstarttests .htm (accessed February 27, 2006).

Bumiller, E. 2003. Bush, to criticism, seeks change in Head Start. *New York Times,* July 8, A1, A18.

Business Roundtable (BRT). 2006. About us. www.businessroundtable.org/aboutUs/Member list.aspx (accessed January 21, 2006).

Callahan, C. 2005. Learner differences. In *Encyclopedia of Education and Human Development, Volume 3,* eds. S. J. Farenga and D. Ness, 775–789. Armonk, NY: M. E. Sharpe.

Cavanagh, S. 2005. Finnish students are at the top of the world class. *Education Week,* March 16, 8.

Dillon, S. 2006. Schools cut back subjects to push reading and math. *New York Times,* March 26, 1, 22.

Economist. 2006. Inequality and the American dream. June 17–23.

Education Week. 2005. *Quality counts 2005: Targeting money toward student performance.* Bethesda, MD: Education Week.

———. 2006a. *Quality counts 2006: A decade of standards-based education.* Bethesda, MD: Education Week.

———. 2006b. Foreseeing errors in test industry. March 1, 18.

———. 2006c. State and district patterns. *Diplomas count: An essential guide to graduation policy and rates.* June 22, 14–15.

Emery, K., and S. Ohanian. 2004. *Why is corporate America bashing our public schools?* Portsmouth, NH: Heinemann.

FairTest. 2004. Joint organizational statement on No Child Left Behind (NCLB) Act. October 21. www.fairtest.org (accessed December 4, 2004).

Finchler, J. 2000. *Testing Miss Malarkey.* New York: Walker & Co.

Goodnight, M. M. 2006. Test time is here. *Alexandria (LA) Town Talk,* March 20. www.thetowntalk.com (accessed March 20, 2006).

Harvard Gazette. 2000. Studies: "High stakes" tests are counterproductive [to] economically disadvantaged students. January 20. www.news.harvard.edu/gazette/2000/01.20/ tests.html (accessed July 4, 2006).

Herring, S. T. 2000. Failure of LEAP test prompts suicide attempt by fifteen-year-old student. *Homer (LA) Guardian-Journal,* October 19, 1, 5.

Herszenhorn, D. M. 2006. For students, figuring out answer sheet was true test. *New York Times,* January 18, B1, B8.

Hirschmann, J. 2004. Letter to Chancellor Joel Klein. Time Out from Testing.org. www.timeoutfromtesting.org/tochancellorklein.php (accessed January 23, 2006).

Jacobson, L. 2004. Pre-K standards said to slight social, emotional skills. *Education Week,* July 14, 13.

Johnson, D. D. and B. Johnson. 2002. *High stakes: Children, testing, and failure in American schools.* Lanham, MD: Rowman & Littlefield.

———. 2006. *High stakes: Poverty, testing, and failure in American schools.* 2d ed. Lanham, MD: Rowman & Littlefield.

Johnson, D. D., B. Johnson, S. Farenga, and D. Ness. 2005. *Trivializing teacher education: The accreditation squeeze.* Lanham, MD: Rowman & Littlefield.

Kirp, D. L. 2006. After the bell curve. *New York Times Magazine,* July 23, 15–16.

Lafayette (LA) Daily Advertiser. 2006. Lafayette school district drops in rank. March 17. www.theadvertiser.com (accessed March 17, 2006).

Louisiana Department of Education. 2004. Gov. Blanco honors schools receiving growth awards. www.doe.state.la.us (accessed January 20, 2005).

Martin Luther King Jr. High School, Sacramento, Calif. www.greatschools.net (accessed July 25, 2006).

Medina, J. and T. Lewin. 2003. High school under scrutiny for giving up on its students. *New York Times,* August 1, B6.

Meier, D. 2004. No politician left behind. *The Nation,* June 14. www.thenation.com/doc/20040614/meier (accessed September 18, 2005).

Meisels, S. J., and S. Atkins-Burnett. 2004. The Head Start National Reporting System: A critique. *Young Children,* January. www.journal.naeyc.org/btj/200401/meisels.asp (accessed February 27, 2006).

Morrison, I. 2006. Classes for overaged students to expand. *Monroe (LA) News Star.* June 4. www.thenewsstar.com (accessed June 4, 2006).

National Commission on Excellence in Education. 1983. *A nation at risk: The imperative for educational reform.* Washington, D.C.: U.S. Government Printing Office.

National Council for Accreditation of Teacher Education (NCATE). n.d. Quick facts about NCATE. www.ncate.org/future/m_future.htm (accessed January 10, 2004).

newdemocracyworld.org. 2002. High stakes testing: Why are they doing this to our kids? newdemocracyworld.org/testing.htm (accessed November 4, 2002).

Noddings, N. 2005. Rethinking a bad law: One scholar's indictment of the No Child Left Behind Act. *Education Week,* February 23, 38.

Olson, L. 2004. NCLB law bestows bounty on test industry. *Education Week,* December 1, 1, 18–19.

Pellegrini, A. D., and C. M. Bohn. 2005. The role of recess in children's cognitive performance and school adjustment. *Educational Researcher,* 34 (1): 13–19.

Rose, L. C., and A. M. Gallup. 2005. The 37th annual Phi Delta Kappa Gallup Poll of the public's attitudes toward the public schools. *Phi Delta Kappan* 86 (September): 41–57.

Saulny, S. 2005. New York plans test to affirm fitness for jobs. *New York Times,* January 29, 1–2.

Sentell, W. 2005. Dropouts up sharply at LA public schools. *Baton Rouge Advocate.* August 17. www.2theadvocate.com (accessed August 17, 2005).

Sorrells, M. 2002. High-threat tests upset N.C. teacher. *Education Week,* September 4, 52–53.

Spellings, M. 2005. Secretary Spellings announces new Commission on the Future of Higher Education. U.S. Department of Education, September 19. www.ed.gov/news/pressreleases/2005/09/09192005.html (accessed March 1, 2006).

Steinhauer, J. 2005. Maybe preschool is the problem: Only four years old, and expelled. *New York Times,* May 22, Section 4.

Sternberg, R. J. 2002. High stakes testing: The good, the bad, and the ugly. Paper presented at Plain Talk Conference, New Orleans, LA, February 19–20.

Time Almanac 2004. 2003. Needham, MA: Pearson Education.

USA Today. 2006. Graduation rates lowest to highest. June 21, 8D.

Walters, A. K., and E. F. Farrell. 2006. College Board takes heat for debacle in SAT scoring. *Chronicle of Higher Education,* March 24, A1, A45.

2

Chronic Racism

THROUGHOUT AMERICAN HISTORY, minorities have not had an easy time of it. Prejudicial actions and low wages have made America's "golden door" difficult for them to open. Ancestral tales speak of non-white, nonnorthern European struggles for equality and a decent life. Most immigrants came to America voluntarily, but one group did not. As revolting as conditions on some immigrant ships were, they were not as inhumane as the slave ships. As paltry as an immigrant's daily wages might have been, they were more than no pay for toiling from sunup to sundown. The laudable accomplishments of African Americans in all arenas are a testament to their indomitability. Although all minority groups have been and continue to be victims of racism, Barnes (2000) notes that blacks are "the most discriminated against and exploited immigrants in the Western world" (7). Their history in America is fraught with glaring and subtle injustices.

Blacks in America: The Colonial Years

Brutality and greed pervade the treatment of blacks in America. In August, 1619, 20 African slaves, owned by a Dutch captain, were sold for supplies to colonists in Jamestown, Virginia. The *Mayflower* had not yet sailed from England. By 1725, the slave population in the colonies had grown to 75,000 (Carruth 1989, 88). Most of that number had been transported from Africa to the Americas on slave ships. Africans sold into slavery were prisoners of ethnic wars or had been kidnapped or orphaned. Others had debts they could not pay (Earle 2000).

A voyage from African to American shores could last as long as 16 weeks. There are eyewitness accounts of the conditions aboard the slavers. In 1788, Alexander Falconbridge wrote about his experiences as a slave ship's physician: "The men, on being brought aboard ship, are immediately fastened together, two and two, by handcuffs on their wrists and by irons riveted on their legs. . . . They are frequently stowed so close as to admit of no other position than lying on their sides" (Dow 2002, 142). Any form of slave resistance, such as refusing to eat, was treated harshly. Dr. Falconbridge recalled, "I have seen coals of fire, glowing hot, put on a shovel and placed so near their lips as to scorch and burn them" (145). Other ship crew members broke the teeth of reluctant eaters and force fed them (Dennis 1984, 22).

When the Atlantic became rough, small "air-ports," that measured only inches in length and width, were closed to keep out the water. The slaves' sources of fresh air were then eliminated. Dr. Falconbridge reported on the effects:

> Some wet and blowing weather having occasioned the port-holes to be shut and the grating to be covered, fluxes and fevers among the negroes ensued. While they were in this situation, I frequently went down among them till at length their rooms became so extremely hot as to be only bearable for a very short time. . . . The deck, that is, the floor of their rooms, was so covered with the blood and mucus which had proceeded from them in consequence of the flux, that it resembled a slaughter-house. (Dow 2002, 146)

Dr. Falconbridge noted that when especially large numbers of slaves were crowded into ships, they "were obliged to lie one upon another" (147). Other eyewitness accounts tell of slaves sitting "one within another's legs, so that each did not occupy more than three feet of space" (201). Under these conditions, from 50 percent to nearly 70 percent of the slaves perished.

> Some captains, to minimize their losses and therefore increase profits, had sick slaves put on rough planks away from the others. Dr. Falconbridge wrote, "By this means those who are emaciated frequently have their skin and even their flesh entirely rubbed off, by the motion of the ship, from the prominent parts of the shoulders, elbows, and hips so as to render the bones quite bare (148).

On May 24, 1829, 41 years after Dr. Falconbridge's account, Robert Walsh boarded a slaver and pirate ship. He recorded the following impressions:

> The slaves were all enclosed under grated hatchways, between decks. The space was so low, that they sat between each other's legs, and stowed so close together, that there was no possibility of their lying down, or at all changing their positions, by night or day. As they belonged to, and were shipped on account of different individuals, they were all branded, like sheep, with the owner's marks of

different forms. . . . The heat of these horrid places was so great, and the odour so offensive, that it was quite impossible to enter them, even had there been room. (Colbert 1997, 136)

Walsh learned that after 17 days at sea, 55 slaves had died because of dysentery and other illnesses. He stated, "While expressing my horror at what I saw, and exclaiming against the state of this vessel for conveying human beings, I was informed by my friends, who had passed so long a time on the coast of Africa, and visited so many ships, that this was one of the best they had seen"(138).

In the years that passed between Dr. Falconbridge's account and that of Robert Walsh, the Declaration of Independence was signed, the Constitution was ratified, and the Bill of Rights was adopted. The colonial elite, especially those in Virginia and Maryland, quickly learned that slave labor was more profitable than the use of indentured servants who, after paying off their debts, were set free. In 1662, the Virginia legislature decreed that a newborn's standing in the colony—that is as a slave or as a free person—depended on the status of the mother. Lyons (2002, 7) points out that the colonists were free to create their own laws because "the British colonies began as private ventures which were chartered by the Crown." The colonists who wrote the laws had a choice, and they chose slavery. No slave had any voice in the legislature, so there was little opposition to these laws. By 1691, the Virginia legislature had "sanctioned the killing of runaway slaves, restricted severely the freeing of slaves, and required that freed slaves be transported out of the colony at the owner's expense" (15).

In 1705, the Virginia General Assembly established a harsh slave code that was emulated by other colonies. It stated that for a major offense such as robbery, "the slave would receive sixty lashes and be placed in stocks, where his or her ears would be cut off, and that for minor offenses, such as associating with whites, slaves would be whipped, branded, or maimed" (*Africans in America* 2005).

When the delegates met in Philadelphia on May 25, 1787, a new Constitution was written after much debate and compromise. It was ratified by the nine required states by June, 1788. Although the word "slavery" was not used by the framers of the Constitution, it is implicit in the "three-fifths clause" (Article I, Section 2, Clause 3) in which "other Persons" (i.e., not free people, indentured servants, or Native Americans) were counted as three-fifths of a person for Congressional representation. Lyons (2002, 17) notes, "While suffrage was denied slaves, their numbers contributed to slaveowners' influence within all three branches of government—not only in Congress but also in the executive branch (as the electoral college reflected congressional representation), and the federal judiciary (selected by the president)." Lyons also points out that this was a curious move by the delegates because slaves were considered property, and no other property was counted for representation. Other proslavery sentiments written into the Constitution were the Fugitive Slave clause that required states to return runaway slaves to their owners, and the extension of slavery for 20 years without interference from Congress.

By the time the delegates to the Constitutional Convention met that May, Vermont, Pennsylvania, Massachusetts, New Hampshire, Connecticut, and Rhode Island had banned slavery or had provided for gradual emancipation. The Northwest Territory, comprising the future states of Wisconsin, Illinois, Indiana, Michigan, and Ohio was designated as free (Earle 2000). This must have been worrisome to the delegates from the South; however, their proslavery stance prevailed. Many legal scholars have argued that Convention delegates from the North gave too much away to Southern interests, and some have questioned how close the Northern delegates' thoughts were to those of the people they represented. Lyons (2002, 22) indicates that "delegates largely represented affluent commercial and plantation interests." He states, "A more representative convention could have endorsed a national program of abolition" (24), but "the Constitution that was agreed upon and ratified accommodated slavery" (25).

Slavery and King Cotton

Northern laws resulted in more free blacks, but discrimination was unconcealed. Earle (2000, 33) writes: "Free blacks always occupied a precarious place in American society, somewhere between slavery and true freedom. Although not legally property, they were perceived by most whites as inferior. . . . For example, Congress barred free blacks from serving in the militia in 1792; 18 years later they were banned from delivering the mail."

Although an act of Congress prohibited additional slaves from entering America after January 1, 1808, by then slavery was firmly entrenched in the South. The act benefited states such as Virginia and Maryland whose tobacco planters had more slaves than they needed. By prohibiting the entry of more African slaves, the planters could sell their own slaves for high prices to the deep southern region.

A 28-year-old teacher and inventor had applied for a patent in 1793 that would spur the need for slave field labor. Eli Whitney's cotton gin, which removed seeds from the fiber of the white bolls, could increase cotton ready for export by nearly fifty-fold. By the third U.S. Census conducted in 1810, the slave population had reached 1,191,364 (Carruth 1989, 214).

Many slave owners worried about slave uprisings. A series of slave revolts, most notably one led by a free black, Denmark Vesey in 1822, and another led by the slave Nat Turner in 1831, rattled southerners. The revolts resulted in the executions of Vesey and Turner and in state slave codes that made it illegal for slaves to gather in groups of six or more, be taught to read or write, own land, keep a dog, and more. Free blacks were not exempt from sections of some state slave codes. In 1848, for example, the *Slave Codes of the State of Georgia* stated that if "free persons of color" traded goods with slaves, they "shall receive on his, her or their bare back or backs, thirty-nine lashes, to be well laid on by a constable of said county, or other person appointed by the justice of the peace for that purpose" (Randall 2005). The 1833 *Digest of the Laws of the State of Alabama* (State of Alabama 2005) contained the following section:

> If any free negro or person of color shall be found in company with any slaves in any kitchen, out-house, or negro-quarter, without a written permission from the owner, master, or overseer of said slaves, said free negro person or person of color shall, for the first offence, receive fifteen lashes, and for every subsequent offence, thirty-nine lashes, on his or her bare back, which may be inflicted by said master, owner, or overseer, or by any officer or member of any patrol company who may find said free negro or person of color, in any kitchen, out-house, or negro-quarter, associating with slaves without such written permission.

The writers of sections of the slave codes apparently feared the influence free blacks might have on slaves to plan their own freedom. Blacks—whether free or in bondage—were even thought to contract a particular disease, *dysaethesia aethiopica*. In 1851, prominent Louisiana physician Dr. Samuel Cartwright wrote that overseers referred to the disease as "rascality." Cartwright, stated that some "ignorantly attribute the symptoms [of the disease] to the debasing influence of slavery on the mind" (*Africans in America* 2005).

Cotton and Cane

The decade leading up to the Civil War is sometimes romanticized as a time of magnolia-scented breezes, moonlit evenings, and fine bourbon sipped on jasmine-entwined verandas. One need only visit Natchez, Mississippi, or travel on Louisiana's River Road to witness the splendor in which some lived. Plantation owners, eager to show off their dazzling wealth, spared no expense on their grand homes. Ceiling artisans specializing in woodworking and plaster trims were brought from Europe, china and glassware were imported from France, mantels were Italian marble, and costly carpets and wallpaper covered floors and walls. There were mahogany staircases, chairs made of ebony with mother-of-pearl inlays, and collections of exquisite porcelain. None of this wealth would have been possible without the unpaid toil of slaves.

Those planters who did not become wealthy from cotton became rich from sugarcane or rice. Nottoway, one of the most enormous of the antebellum planters' homes, and still standing, has 53,000 square feet. This Louisiana mansion has 64 rooms, 5 magnificent galleries, and overlooks the Mississippi. An elegant all-white ballroom, a library filled with leather-bound books, and a pillared hall awaited visitors to the estate. The family's children were schooled by German music teachers, a French art teacher, and were watched over by an English governess. The principal crop grown in Nottoway fields was sugarcane, and the plantation had 500 slaves to do the work. This left ample time for the family to engage in socializing. In a history of Nottoway, Ailenroc (1903, 51) writes: "They were social and fond of giving dinners, in which they excelled; fish, ice, and oysters in season being sent from New Orleans regularly, with other good things." Kate Stone lived on her family's antebellum cotton plantation, Brokenburn, in northeastern Louisiana. The plantation had 150 slaves. Stone recalled, "It required quite a corps of servants to keep us well waited on at Brokenburn, for no one expected to wait on himself" (Anderson 1972, 8).

Slavery was lucrative for dealers as well as plantation owners. In the antebellum South, there were two million slave sales (Johnson 1999). A healthy young adult male slave could bring as much as $2,000 to his owner—over $42,000 in today's money. Erickson (1997, 7) writes, "Slave dealers could make large amounts of money: Each of the partners in the firm of Franklin & Armfield, one of the largest in the business, had made of a profit of more than $500,000 [about $8,925,000 today] by the time he retired." At slave auctions, little or no effort was made to keep black families together. Owners, buyers, and traders considered slaves a commodity and some recorded the births of slaves on their plantations under the category, "Stock" (Dennis 1984). Some slave owners "freed" their slaves when they got too old, weak, or sick to work and there would be no monetary advantage in keeping them. Other slaves were used as currency. Johnson (1999) reports that a child was separated from his mother "and used by a slave trader to pay a bar bill" (42). Field hands worked from daybreak to nightfall. House slaves were on call 24 hours a day. Even though the house slaves were considered to have a somewhat easier life than the field slaves, their work was labor intensive. For example, when ordered to wash a party dress, the slaves had to first remove the buttons and lace and then sew these back on when the dress was dry (Isaacs 2000). House slaves were subjected to the same whippings and tortures meted out to those who worked in the fields.

No free person can understand what it is like to be considered another person's property. No free person can understand the omnipresent fear of being sold away from one's family, the humiliation of being handled on the auction block by potential buyers, the beatings, mutilations, and endless toil. Slaves were forced to work when they were ill. On some rice plantations in the Deep South, child mortality rate was as high as 90 percent (*Africans in America* 2005). Clothing was handed out once a year, and shoes had to be stuffed with rags to keep feet warm in the winter. Some slaves were not issued shoes, and in the winter, their feet would "crack open" (Federal Writers' Project 1941). Slaves who worked in the fields on large plantations were watched and prodded by a slave driver and an overseer. If a slave picked dirty cotton, he or she could receive 20 lashes with a whip, and if a slave did not pick the expected amount of cotton in a day, he or she could receive 40 lashes (Erickson 1997, 27). House slaves reported being burned with a hot iron as a form of discipline, being whipped for something as minor as an overbaked dinner roll, or being forced to walk several times through hot coals because chickens got too close to a fire a slave was tending (Federal Writers' Project 1941). Slaves were not allowed to leave the plantation without a pass from their owners. Patrollers, or "paddy rollers" were white men who hunted down runaway slaves and checked for slaves' passes if they were off their home plantations. Former slaves reported that punishments by the patrollers for not having a pass ranged from beatings to murder.

Former Slaves Speak

The closest free people can get to even a notion of slavery's abominations is to read narratives of former slaves. There were only about 150 slave narratives that were published before 1930 (Howard University 2005). In 1929, Fisk University in Nashville and Southern University in Baton Rouge started interviewing former slaves. During the Great Depression, unemployed writers, through the federal Works Progress Administration (WPA), were hired to interview ex-slaves. Between 1936 and 1938, 2,300 interviews were conducted. They comprise *Born in Slavery: Slave Narratives from the Federal Writers' Project* which now is in the Library of Congress. Although the WPA collection is valuable, the interviews from the Fisk University project are considered to be even more so. Sutcliffe (2000) points out:

> In particular, the interviewees in the Fisk University project were more outspoken, on the whole, than the WPA subjects about the cruelties they endured under slavery. One possible reason is that Fisk interviews were conducted by Ophelia Settle Egypt, a Howard University graduate who was working for Dr. Charles Johnson, a professor in Fisk's Social Sciences Department. Both were black, and it is possible that the former slaves felt comfortable relating their experiences to a black professional woman who encouraged them to speak about

their experiences, good and bad. . . . By contrast, most of the WPA interviewers were white women from the middle and upper classes in communities where the interviews were conducted. (ix, x)

One must also remember that the interviews of the former slaves living in the South were taken before the civil rights movement, so there might have been a fear for their lives at a time when lynchings of blacks were not uncommon. The following voices from former slaves are written exactly as they were typed by the WPA interviewers (Federal Writers' Project 1941). Some of the interviewers transposed the interviewees' dialect into "standard" English. Others tried to represent the slaves' dialect and typed, for example, *ag'in* for *again*, *wid* for *with*, *dey* for *they*. Racism among the interviewers appears in how some of the slaves were addressed. Adeline Willis was called "Aunt Adeline" by her interviewer, and Robert Falls was referred to as "Uncle Robert" by the woman who interviewed him although neither former slave was related to the WPA interviewers. Tom Mills was referred to by his interviewer as "Uncle Tom Mills" who "is one of the most contented old darkies surviving the good old days when range was open and a livelihood was the easiest thing in the world to get." Despite the aforementioned drawbacks, the following voices of former slaves give us some inkling, however small, of what those living in bondage had to endure.

John W. Fields, an ex-slave born in Kentucky, recalled:

There was 11 other children besides myself in my family. When I was six years old, all of us children were taken from my parents, because my master died and his estate had to be settled. We slaves were divided by this method. Three disinterested persons were chosen to come to the plantation and together they wrote the names of the different heirs on a few slips of paper. These slips were put in a hat and passed among us slaves. Each took out a slip and the name on the slip was the new owner. . . . I can't describe the heartbreak and horror of that separation. I was only six years old. . . . Twelve children taken from my mother in one day.

Fields also recalled:

In most of us colored folks was the great desire to [be] able to read and write. We took advantage of every opportunity to educate ourselves. The greater part of the plantation owners were very harsh if we were caught trying to learn or write. It was the law that if a white man was caught trying to educate a negro slave, he was liable to prosecution entailing a fine of fifty dollars and a jail sentence. . . . Our ignorance was the greatest hold the South had on us.

Delia Garlic, a former slave born in Virginia, told her interviewer about being sold to slave speculators. She said:

Course dey cry; you think dey not cry when dey was sold lak cattle? I could tell you 'bout it all day, but even den you couldn't guess de awfulness of it. It's bad to belong to folks dat own you soul an' body; dat can tie you up to a tree, wid yo' face to de tree an' yo' arms fastened tight aroun' it; who take a long curlin' whip an' cut de blood ever' lick. Folks a mile away could hear dem awful whip-pings. . . . Us didn't know nothin' 'cept to work. Us was up by three or four in de mornin' an' everybody got dey somthin' to eat in de [plantation] kitchen. Dey didn't give us no way to cook, nor nothin' to cook in our cabins. Soon as us dressed us went by de kitchen an' got our piece of cornbread. Dey wasn't even no salt in dem las' years. Dat piece of cornbread was all us had for breakfas', an' for supper, us had de same.

William Moore, a former slave born in Selma, Alabama, was interviewed at the age of 83. He remembered:

My mammy had a terrible bad back once. I seen her tryin' to git the clothes off her back and a woman say, "What's the matter with you back?" It was raw and bloody and she say Marse Tom done beat her with a handsaw with the teeth to her back. She died with the marks on her, the teeth holes goin' crosswise her back. When I's growed I asks her 'bout it and she say Marse Tom got mad at the cookin' and grabs her by the hair and drug her out the house and grabs the saw off the tool bench and whips her.

Sarah Benjamin, a former slave born in Louisiana was one of "60 or 70" slaves on a plantation. She recalled: "Dey didn't larn us nothin' and iffen you did larn to write, you better keep it to yourse'f cause some slaves Cot [got] de thumb or finger cut off for larnin' to write." Former slave H. B. Holloway also told of severe punishment handed out by owners if a slave attempted to write. Holloway said, "If he catch his slaves toying with the pencil, why, he cut off one of their fingers." Charley Mitchell, a former slave in Virginia, said that if a slave had learned to write just some initials on a barn door with a piece of charcoal, the white owners would "cut his fingers off."

Robert Falls, who lived with 15 other slaves in a cabin on a North Carolina plantation, told his interviewer that the animals were fed better than the slaves. Even if some slaves had been treated less cruelly and violently than oth-ers, they were always aware that they were someone's property and could be sold for a variety of reasons: a master's unpaid debts, a master's death, or as punishment. Falls said, "If I had my life to live over, I would die fighting rather than be a slave again." Tom Robinson's mother was sold away from him before the age of 11, and he had been owned by three different masters before he reached 15 years of age. Mr. Robinson stated: "You can take anything. No mat-ter how good you treat it—it wants to be free. You can treat it good and feed it good and give it everything it seems to want—but if you open the cage—it's happy." There was resistance from some slaves against their masters. Slaves sometimes intentionally worked slowly when the overseer wasn't watching; others sabotaged machinery or tried to ruin crops (*Africans in America* 2005). Resistance came at a terrible price, however. W. B. Allen, a former slave from Georgia, recalled that he had seen slaves beaten to death for minor "offenses" such as "Talking back to—'sassing'—a white person" and for "Loitering on their work" (Federal Writers' Project 1941). Despite attempts to change their lot, most slaves had few avenues of escape. Some did manage to run away, but many were caught and returned to their owners. Tales of the Underground Railroad abound, but as Earle (2000) points out, stations in the South, where the bulk of the slave population lived, were few. There were valiant efforts by Harriet Tubman, a slave who escaped to freedom, and the Northern Quakers who were a vital part of the Railroad, to help Southern slaves. The odds of successfully leaving bondage, however, were slim. Just to get beyond the plantation was a terrifying proposition. Henry Waldon, a former Mississippi slave, remembered that an owner would:

> Send for a man that had hounds to track you if you run away. . . . Them hounds would worry you and bite you and have you bloody as a beef, but you dassent hit one of them. . . . They wouldn't try to keep the hounds off of you; they would set them on you to see them bite you. Five or six or seven hounds bitin' you on every side and a man settin' on a horse holding a doubled shotgun on you. (Federal Writers' Project 1941)

Most Southerners did not own slaves, and those who owned more than 20 slaves comprised only about 6.5 percent of the South's population (Erickson 1997, 10). This small, wealthy percentage had a great deal of power, but one might wonder why the majority of the population did not try to outlaw slavery. Some historians believe that poorer whites in the region wanted to emulate the successful planters and hoped to own many slaves themselves one day. Others believe that some poor whites used slavery as an excuse to "look down on" a group of people and therefore raise their own status.

Reconstruction

In 1865, the Civil War ended, and the Thirteenth Amendment was ratified which freed four million slaves. Some plantation families were abusive at just the mention of freedom. Others did not immediately tell their slaves about their freedom. Former slave Robert Barr recalled a slave who learned of his imminent freedom. Barr said, "His young mistress heard em say he was going to be free and she walked up . . . and spit in his face." Former Louisiana slave

William Mathews remembered, "We went right on workin' after freedom. Old Buck Adams wouldn't let us go." Tempie Cummins related that her mother had overheard her owners talk about the slaves being free, but that they were not going to tell them until they made "another crop or two." Susan Merritt said that her owner made the slaves work several months after freedom and promised them 20 acres and a mule—which they did not receive. She also recalled that "lots" of slaves were killed after they were set free "'cause the slaves in Harrison County turn loose right at freedom and them in Rusk County wasn't. But they hears 'bout it and runs away to freedom in Harrison County and they owners have 'em bushwhacked, that [is] shot down" (Federal Writers' Project 1941).

Former slaves who left the plantation had little to help them in a new life— no education, no money, few possessions. Henry Waldon stated, "None of the masters never give me anything. None of them as I knows of never give anything to any of the slaves when they freed 'em." Ex-slave Anna Miller told her interviewer that when freedom came, her owner told the slaves, "'All dat wants to go, git now. You has nothin'.' And he turns dem away, nothin' on 'cept old rags. 'Twarn't enough to cover dere body. No hat, no shoes, no unnerwear" (Federal Writers' Project 1941). Charley Mitchell said:

> After surrender a man calls a meetin' of all the slaves in the fairgrounds and tells us we's free. We wasn't promised anything. We jus' had to do the best we could. But I heared lots of slaves what lived on farms say they's promised forty acres and a mule but they never did git it. We had to go to work for whatever they'd pay us, and we didn't have nothing and no place to go when we was turned loose, but down the street and road.

Annie Osborne, a former slave in Louisiana, recollected, "My white folks didn't teach us nothin' 'cept how they could put the whip on us," and that her master "wouldn't let us go after surrender." She and her mother, while making soap, ran away from the plantation while the pot still boiled. Van Moore remembered that when freedom came, his mother was told by the plantation owner's wife, "'You is free now, and you all jus' have to do the best you kin.'" Moore also recalled that when his father was set free, he had nothing—"not even a shirt" (Federal Writers' Project 1941).

Many ex-slaves had little choice but to remain on the plantation and work as sharecroppers; that is, they would receive a portion of their harvest as payment for their work. Sometimes they received nothing for their labor because the plantation owner charged exorbitant amounts for tools, clothing, and the same housing they had as slaves. As Katie Rowe recalled, "But we all gits fooled on dat first go-out! When de crop all in we don't git half! Old Mistress sick in town, and de overseer was still on de place and he charge us half de crop for de quarters [housing] and de mules and tools and grub!" (Federal Writers' Project 1941).

Lyons (2002, 36) points out that from 1862 to 1872, the U.S. government gave "more than a hundred million acres of public land, plus many millions of dollars, to railroad companies," and in 1866, one year after the end of the Civil War, "gave millions of acres of mineral-rich public lands to mining companies." There was free land for railroad and mining barons but no free land for those who toiled for years as slaves. Lyons notes that during this era, freedmen had difficulty getting credit and had to pay twice as much as whites for a piece of land. Wealth and political power remained in the hands of the planters just as it did before the Civil War.

The Freedmen's Bureau was created in 1865 to help newly freed African Americans, but a month after Abraham Lincoln was assassinated, his successor, Andrew Johnson of Tennessee proclaimed that "white men alone must govern the South" (Earle 2000, 66). Congress passed the Fourteenth and Fifteenth Amendments that gave citizenship to freed slaves and gave former male slaves the right to vote. Between 1865 and 1877, several African American males were elected to state positions, and 16 were elected to Congress. This progress angered white supremacists who began chipping away at political progress made by blacks. Poll taxes, hidden balloting sites, literacy tests, and fear were used to keep blacks from voting. The Ku Klux Klan, formed in Pulaski, Tennessee, in 1865, was especially known for its strong-arm tactics in trying to return the South to white-only rule. Lynchings in the South were not uncommon. Earle (2000) states that 3,200 Southern blacks were lynched between 1880 and 1930. Most of these lynchings occurred in Alabama, Georgia, Louisiana, Mississippi, and Texas. Lyons (2002, 29–30) writes: "Many lynchings were public, and many were publicized in advance. Photographs of victims, participants, and spectators were widely circulated, some on printed postcards sent through the U.S. mail. Antilynching legislation, frequently proposed, never made it through both houses of Congress. White supremacy was thus violently re-established."

Even a goal as noble as establishing schools for former plantation workers met with opposition. Edmonia G. Highgate was a teacher working in Louisiana for the American Missionary Association in 1866. Highgate wrote: "Twice I have been shot at in my room. My night school scholars have been shot but none killed. A week ago an aged freedman just across the way was shot so badly as to break his arm and leg" (Sterling 1976, 20).

In the same year, a New Orleans newspaper stated:

The citizens have opposed by all means in their power the continuance of the great work of education in the country parishes [counties]. They have refused to rent buildings for school purposes and to board the teachers. They have whipped Mr. LeBlanc at Point Coupee; dangerously stabbed in the back Mr. Burnham at Monroe; and beaten almost to death Mr. Ruby at Jackson. The record of the teachers of the first colored schools in Louisiana will be one of honor and blood. (Sterling 1976, 21)

Homer Plessy was 30 years old when he was jailed for sitting in a Louisiana railroad car designated for whites only. His case made it to the U.S. Supreme Court in 1896; the judges voted in favor of the railroad. The Court's "separate but equal" stance defined the next era of mistreatment of blacks in America.

Jim Crow

The Jim Crow laws were named after a minstrel character's song, "Jump Jim Crow" (Davis 2005). The Jim Crow portion of the song's title eventually was transferred to a racist portrayal of a black character played by white men in blackface. The Jim Crow laws were designed to separate the races in public areas such as restaurants, parks, theaters, trains, hotels, taxi stands, and hospitals. Blacks were expected to move off sidewalks to let whites pass and drinking fountains were marked "Colored" and "For Whites Only." African Americans knew that they were not welcome in places of business owned by whites, and if they did venture into such stores, they were waited on last and often told the store didn't carry their sizes. By 1900, Tennessee, Mississippi, Louisiana, Virginia, Georgia, North Carolina, South Carolina, Arkansas, Alabama, Florida, and Texas had Jim Crow laws on the books. Even some courthouse entrances and exits were designated "For Whites Only" (Davis 2005). Sadie Delany (Delany, Delany, and Hearth 1993), an African American living in North Carolina during this time, remembered, "We knew we were already second-class citizens, but those Jim Crow laws set it in stone" (63).

The "equal" in "separate but equal" was open to interpretation. Chafe, Gavins, and Korstad (2001, 153) point out: "The lessons that Jim Crow taught to black children were numerous and easy to comprehend. Children learned that they were not allowed to attend the same schools as whites. After a short while they saw that only white children received a bus to ride to and from school, along with new books and desks. They learned too that only white students had decent libraries or science labs." Those who recalled going to school during Jim Crow spoke of no teacher supplies in the classrooms, six- or seven-mile walks to school when a white elementary school might be a block or two away, and buildings without heat during cold winter weather—even though their families paid local taxes. They remembered white children in schoolbuses taunting them and hurling stones and garbage at them. (See Chafe, Gavins, and Korstad [2001] for oral histories of those who lived under Jim Crow laws.)

Racism also existed in America outside the former Confederacy. For example, approximately 400,000 African Americans served during World War I, but they were not allowed to join the Marines or become naval officers. In 1939, the Daughters of the American Revolution (DAR) would not allow Marian Anderson, a well-known black soprano, to sing in Constitution Hall. African American blood donated to the American Red Cross blood banks was kept separate from blood donated by whites until the 1940s (Dennis 1984). After World War II, the nation's attention was turned to heroism that ushered in the civil rights movement.

The Second Reconstruction

The period after World War II often is referred to as "The Second Reconstruction." Actions during the war such as those by Dorie Miller, an African American from Waco, Texas, shamed politicians into reexamining the segregation of blacks in the military. Miller was a Ship's Cook Third Class on the USS *West Virginia* when it was hit on December 7, 1941 in Pearl Harbor. Under attack by Japanese bombs and torpedoes, Miller, without training, operated an antiaircraft gun to defend the ship. He later lost his life from a Japanese torpedo in another naval incident where 646 U.S. servicemen died. Miller received the Navy Cross after his courageous actions in Pearl Harbor, and, according to the Department of the Navy's Historical Center, he was "entitled to the Purple Heart Medal; the American Defense Service Medal; Fleet Clasp; the Asiatic-Pacific Campaign Medal; and the World War II Victory Medal" (Naval Historical Center 2001).

As the Cold War descended, the Soviet Union used America's treatment of blacks as a propaganda tool (Lyons 2002). This served as a wake-up call to some politicians who previously had given little thought to race relations or supported the status quo.

The National Association for the Advancement of Colored People (NAACP), founded in 1909, was instrumental in bringing school segregation to the forefront. By 1952, The Supreme Court had on its docket cases from four states and the District of Columbia regarding the segregation of American schools. The Court, to simplify matters, combined the cases under *Oliver Brown et al. v. the Board of Education of Topeka.* Oliver Brown was a welder and assistant minister and the only male plaintiff in a lawsuit against the Topeka, Kansas, Board of Education. He and 12 other parents, supported by the Topeka NAACP, argued for integration of the city's schools. The parents lost their case in the U.S. District Court, but on May 17, 1954, the Supreme Court outlawed the "separate but equal" practice among public schools and ordered their desegregation (NAACP 2005).

The *Brown* decision was met with strong resistance from segregationists. Editorials in major Southern newspapers such as the *Jackson* (MS) *Daily News* decried the decision and stated that it would not be followed. In Prince Edward County, Virginia, the board of supervisors, rather than integrating the public schools, withheld funding from all the public schools. The schools stayed closed for five years (U.S. Department of the Interior 2005). Boger and Orfield (2005) pointed out that although the *Brown* decision offered promise to African American children, in practice, the desegregation of schools was to be "locally designed" (4). They state, "Only 1 percent of black students in the South were in majority white schools in the summer of 1963" (5). This was nine years after the *Brown* decision. Boger and Orfield noted that desegregation was not taken seriously, however, until the Civil Rights Act of 1964 was signed by President Lyndon Johnson. Even then, civil rights were not taken to heart by everyone. One day after the Civil Rights Act was signed, for example, Lester Maddox, who owned a chicken restaurant in Atlanta, brandished a pistol when African Americans tried to enter his eatery. He also gave white customers in his restaurant ax handles to further clarify his segregationist stance. In 1967, this same Lester Maddox was elected governor of Georgia.

Individual and collective acts of heroism preceded and followed civil rights legislation. Rosa Parks, arrested and fined in 1955 when she refused to give up her Montgomery, Alabama, bus seat to a white man, was the inspiration for a citywide bus boycott. In 1960, four students from the North Carolina Agricultural and Technical College ordered coffee at a "whites only" lunch counter. James Meredith was the first African American to attend classes at the all-white University of Mississippi. It took the deployment of federal troops to ensure that the nine-year Air Force veteran could attend classes. In 1965 Dr. Martin Luther King Jr. led a march from Selma to Montgomery, Alabama, to rally for voting rights. On the final day of the march, Ku Klux Klan members shot and killed Viola Gregg Liuzzo. Names well-known and names lost to all but those who knew them mark the timeline in the struggle for equal rights (Earle 2000).

Incidents of racism and insensitivity are not difficult to find today. In the fall of 2005, obscenities were spray-painted on the single black fraternity house on the Louisiana State University (LSU) campus while its members were at a meeting to promote unity among minority students. In response to the vandalism, African American students marched to the football stadium on game day to protest the display of purple-and-gold Confederate flags by fans and tailgaters. The protest set off a slew of comments from those who fly the Confederate flag in LSU colors. Jacobs (2005) reports:

> Bob Kane, who was tailgaiting under a purple-and-gold Confederate flag with an LSU Tiger logo, said he didn't see what the protesting students were so upset about. . . . John Lally and Bryan Dupont were also tailgaiting under a purple-and-gold Confederate flag. "It's part of my freedom of speech. I can fly whatever flag I want," Lally said. "If you don't like it, get out of the South."

An African American student, "Jillian," wrote a comment to the online version of *The Daily Reveille*, LSU's student newspaper. The comment stated, in part, "white people will never understand what it is like to look at some fabric with some shapes and colors and have a burning lump rise in their throat and a knot form in their belly." "RE" from Dallas, Texas, also submitted a comment to *The Reveille*: "Where can I go to get my LSU Rebel flag?"

Briscoe and Thomas (2005, 41) found that there were six racist incidents in one week "at or around" the University of Virginia in the fall of 2005: "Black students also reported racial slurs shouted from passing cars and trucks and written on a birthday card attached to an apartment door."

A Georgia television station (WSBTV.com 2005) reports that "racist graffiti that contained references to the Ku Klux Klan . . . and a crude picture of gallows" were found at an elementary school in Kennesaw, Georgia. In Coushatta, Louisiana, black children were ordered to sit in the back of a school bus while their white classmates rode in the front seats. The white bus driver was suspended and then allowed to retire. A NAACP spokesperson noted, "At this point, it is extremely alarming. We fought that battle 50 years ago, and we won. Why is this happening again?" (Welborn 2006).

Racism also blights other regions of the United States. An interracial Long Island, New York couple recently relocated to North Carolina after receiving a series of hate mailings. Their nine-year-old daughter was so fearful after the incidents that "she didn't want to get on the school bus in the morning" (Vargas 2005, A5). The University of Chicago's student newspaper, the *Chicago Maroon*, reported that a party, with the theme "Straight-Thuggin Ghetto Party," was held in a campus dormitory (Michaels 2005). In a letter to the University's administration, the political chair of the Organization of Black Students wrote that partygoers were "performing derisive stereotypes commonly associated with impoverished Black communities (i.e., urban 'ghettos') for the purpose of mocking a disadvantaged group of human beings." A racist "Halloween in the Hood," fraternity party at Johns Hopkins University featured a pirate skeleton hanging from a noose and partygoers who were invited to wear "bling bling, ice ice, grills, and hoochie hoops" (Reddy 2006).

Marie Samuelson was born and grew up in a small, segregated town near Mobile, Alabama. She has worked as a teacher and librarian in Ohio and in New York. In an interview recently conducted by the authors, Ms. Samuelson relayed her encounters with racism when seeking to dine in restaurants, while shopping, in school, and in her employment.

Dining in a restaurant: In Alabama, blacks were not welcomed in restaurants. The practice was segregation in-the-raw. . . . In Ohio, on several occasions, I experienced waiting at my table for long periods of time and seeing white customers arriving afterwards served ahead of me. A more recent incident occurred at a Long Island restaurant in 2005. My husband made reservations a couple of weeks in advance for 6:00 P.M. dinner. He and I arrived at 5:45 P.M. Upon arrival, he reminded the hostess that we had reservations for a group of seven and stated the time. Everything appeared in order as we waited near the entrance. By 6:00 P.M., all of our guests had arrived. At 6:15 P.M., we had not been seated. My husband inquired and was told they were getting the table ready. At 6:30 P.M., we were told very casually, by one of the hostesses, that our table had been given to a group of ladies who arrived earlier and decided they would all like to be seated together. It was suggested that we go upstairs and find seating or we could wait until the ladies were finished.

Shopping: As a child growing up in the South, it was understood that blacks went to the end of the line. Once in line, whites were permitted to cut in front continuously. . . . From a very young age, I questioned my mother as to why we could not cut lines at school and yet when we went to the store, people always cut in front of us. My mother always responded angrily, "I wish you would stop asking me that same question over and over. That's the way it is, and you might as well get used to it." As I became older, I stopped asking that question. I began to understand what was happening. It made me feel sad and bitter inside. I also understood something else; my mother's angry response had not really been directed at me. It was directed at the system. Repeating my tired question merely gave her an opportunity to vent some of her hurt and frustration.

Through the years, I have experienced acts of discrimination many times while shopping. Most recently, it took place at Macy's on Long Island. I countered it with a technique that gives me a bit of satisfaction although it does not solve the problem. When I have the time, I wait while the cashier pretends that she does not see me and discriminately waits on whites. When she (most cases have been females) can no longer ignore me and makes her initial approach, I make eye contact, hold the item, and state, "I was interested in purchasing this item, but since I was ignored for so long, I have decided to let you keep it and take my business elsewhere." I place the item on the counter and walk away.

In school: Over the years, I watched so many black students punished unfairly in the school system, especially black males. Ninety percent of the time if fights erupted between black and white males, the white assistant principal would give the white males fewer suspension days than the black males. There were occasions when white males received no time out of school. The black child always bore the blame for starting the incident no matter how many witnesses stated otherwise. Even when the black child had been called a "nigger," still they were punished more severely for not controlling their anger. Naturally, when the white child was called "honky," the guilty black child was punished severely again. Each situation was no-win for black students.

Getting a job: I was informed by a friend that a position had become available at a junior high school in a predominantly white community. There was a major problem. The white parents did not want a black librarian, the retiring white librarian did not want a black in the position, and the white supervisor did not want a black (it was common knowledge that the supervisor hired as few blacks as possible). . . . I received a call from the principal offering me the position. He said, "You have spunk! I like that because you will need it here." And need it, I did!

When I reported for my first day of work, which was two weeks before the teachers and students, I was greeted with an unexpected surprise. I opened the library office, which was a large room. The floor was filled with card files, magazines, books, bookends—everything one could associate with operating a library. It appeared that all had been deliberately dumped on the floor. Seeing this, I decided to survey the shelves. As I expected, books were intentionally mixed, shelf after shelf, as though the Dewey Decimal System did not exist. I did not panic, I went straight to the principal. He was appalled after viewing the situation. He advised me to take whatever time I needed to get the library back in order.

As the new librarian, I was tested thoroughly. White parents were up-in-arms and complained that the library was not the same because I refused to cancel out teachers and classes so that parents could have meetings and drink coffee when there were other places to meet in the building. White students wrote "nigger" in large letters on sheets of paper and left them on tables for me to see. Sometimes it was misspelled "niger." Nazi symbols were drawn on the sign-in sheets on the library counter. "Nigger librarian" was written and left sticking out on bookshelves. I overheard several white boys saying they knew which car I drove. I said nothing. I shared my concern with the head custodian who was white and one of his black assistants. They assured me that no one would touch my car and no one did. These two men became my dear friends.

White teachers sent me messages carried by white students asking me if I knew who they were. And if I didn't, I had better learn that they came when they wanted to. No one was going to tell them when they could bring their class to the library. I never responded to such unprofessional tactics. In a staff meeting, I addressed all the issues briefly. I made it clear that I ran an equal opportunity library with rules and that everyone would be treated fairly and must abide by them. I further clarified that they did not have to like me, but I demanded the same respect from them that they received from me. When I sat, there was silence.

Benjamin is a 15-year-old white freshman who attends a public school of high socioeconomic status on Long Island. When interviewed and asked if he had seen racial discrimination in his school or community, Benjamin replied, "Yes, actually, just a few weeks ago this group of kids was making fun of an African American kid during lunch in the cafeteria. They kept calling him a slave and telling him to get things for them. The one kid that was getting picked on stood up and starting fighting. The teachers broke it up and I think all of them were suspended."

Harrington (1962, 146) writes, "There has never been a disability in American society to equal racial prejudice. It is the most effective single instrument for keeping people down that has ever been found." More than 45 years later, his statements hold.

Lyons (2002, 41–42) points out:

> After three hundred and fifty years of slavery and Jim Crow, African Americans entered the Second Reconstruction with wealth, income, and life prospects disproportionately lower than that of their White peers. Despite less overt discrimination and more school and job opportunities, that deficit remains substantial. . . . As the recent Luxembourg Income Study shows, whereas America's rich are the richest in the Western world, its poor are among the poorest. And the children among America's poor, mostly Black or Hispanic, are the very poorest.

In the following chapter we examine the legacy of discrimination and how it has affected the excluded class whose children must take the same high-stakes tests as children of the affluent.

References

Africans in America. 2005. Public Broadcasting Service Online. www.pbs.org/wgbh/aia/ (accessed October 17, 2005).

Ailenroc, M. R. 1903. *The White Castle of Louisiana.* Louisville, KY: John P. Morton.

Anderson, J. Q., ed. 1972. *Brokenburn: The journal of Kate Stone 1861–1868.* Baton Rouge: Louisiana State University Press.

Barnes, A. S. 2000. *Everyday racism: A book for all Americans.* Naperville, IL: Sourcebooks, Inc.

Boger, J. C., and G. Orfield, eds. 2005. *School resegregation: Must the South turn back?* Chapel Hill: University of North Carolina Press.

Briscoe, D., and E. Thomas. 2005. Hate on campus: The University of Virginia rallies against racism. *Newsweek,* November 28, 41.

Carruth, G. 1989. *What happened when: A chronology of life and events in America.* New York: Harper & Row.

Chafe, W. H., R. Gavins, and R. Korstad, eds. 2001. *Remembering Jim Crow: African Americans tell about life in the segregated South.* New York: New Press in Association with Lyndhurst Books of the Center for Documentary Studies of Duke University.

Colbert, D., ed. 1997. *Eyewitness to America: 500 years of America in the words of those who saw it happen.* New York: Pantheon Books.

Daily Reveille (Louisiana State University, Baton Rouge). 2005. Fans continue to fly Rebel flag. October 17. www.lsureveille.com/vfeedback (accessed October 26, 2005 and November 21, 2005).

Davis, R. L. F. 2005. Creating Jim Crow: In-depth essay. www.jimcrowhistory.org (accessed November 16, 2005).

Delany, S., A. E. Delany, and A. H. Hearth. 1993. *Having our say: The Delany Sisters' first 100 years.* New York: Kodansha International.

Dennis, D. 1984. *Black history for beginners.* New York: Writers and Readers Publishing.

Dow, G. F. 2002. *Slave ships and slaving.* Mineola, NY: Dover Publications.

Earle, J. 2000. *The Routledge atlas of African American history.* New York: Routledge.

Erickson, P. 1997. *Daily life on a Southern plantation 1853.* New York: Puffin.

Federal Writers' Project. 1941. *Born in Slavery: Slave narratives from the Federal Writers' Project, 1936–1938.* Library of Congress American Memory collections. memory .loc.gov/ammem/snhtml/snhome.html (accessed November 6, 2005).

Harrington, M. 1962. *The other America: Poverty in the United States.* New York: Simon & Schuster, 1993.

Howard University. 2005. Slave narratives. www.founders.howard.edu/Reference/ Webliographies/slavenarrativeswpic/ (accessed November 5, 2005).

Isaacs, S. S. 2000. *Picture the past: Life on a Southern plantation.* Chicago, IL: Heinemann.

Jacobs, D. 2005. LSU students protest display of Confederate flag. *Baton Rouge Advocate,* October 23, 2005. www.2theadvocate.com/stories/102305/new_protest—1.shtml (accessed November 23, 2005).

Johnson, W. 1999. *Soul by soul: Life inside the antebellum slave market.* Cambridge, MA: Harvard University Press.

Lyons, D. 2002. Unfinished business: Racial junctures in US history and their legacy. Boston University School of Law Working Paper Series. www.bu.edu/law/faculty/ papers/pdf_files/LyonsD061702.pdf (accessed October 23, 2005).

Michaels, T. 2005. "Ghetto"-themed dorm party offends students. *Chicago Maroon,* October 25. maroon.uchicago.edu/news/articles/ (accessed June 25, 2006).

National Association for the Advancement of Colored People (NAACP). 2005. *Timeline.* www.naacp.org/about/about_history.html (accessed November 20, 2005).

Naval Historical Center. 2001. Ship's Cook Third Class Doris Miller, USN. www.history .navy.mil/faqs/faq57-4.htm (accessed November 20, 2005).

Randall, V. R., ed. 2005. Slave code of the State of Georgia, 1848. University of Dayton. academic.udayton.edu/race/02rights/slavelaw.htm (accessed October 17, 2005).

Reddy, S. 2006. Hopkins targets campus racism. *Baltimore Sun,* November 3. www .baltimoresun.com (accessed November 3, 2006).

State of Alabama. 2005. A digest of the laws of the State of Alabama—1833: Compiled under the authority of the General Assembly by John G. Aiken. www.archives.state .al.us/teacher/slavery/lesson1/doc1.html (accessed October 18, 2005).

Sterling, D., ed. 1976. *The trouble they seen: The story of reconstruction in the words of African Americans.* New York: De Capo Press.

Sutcliffe, A., ed. 2000. *Mighty rough times, I tell you: Personal accounts of slavery in Tennessee.* Winston-Salem, NC: John F. Blair.

U.S. Department of the Interior. 2005. National Park Service: *Brown v. Board of Education.* www.nps.gov/brvb/ (accessed November 20, 2005).

Vargas, T. 2005. Refugees from racism. *Newsday.* August 12, A5.

WSBTV.com. 2005. Teens arrested in racial graffiti case. www.wsbtv.com/print/5524422/detail.html (accessed March 24, 2007).

Welborn, V. 2006. Red River parish school bus driver made black children sit in back of the bus. *Alexandria (LA) Town Talk,* August 24, 2006. www.thetowntalk.com (accessed August 24, 2006).

3

The Excluded Class:
Poverty, Race, and Social Class

The Hidden New Orleans

HURRICANE KATRINA WILL BE REMEMBERED as the storm that nearly destroyed one of America's favorite Southern cities, New Orleans, and parts of the Gulf Coast. Before August 29, 2005, New Orleans was the place to let loose and listen to music such as Dixieland jazz, zydeco, and swamp pop. New Orleans and all of Louisiana and neighboring coastal Mississippi were places to find some of the tastiest and most varied food in the United States. New Orleans restaurants, including Brennan's, Galatoire's, and Commander's Palace, are legendary. The mom-and-pop Cajun or soul food cafes that serve bodacious chicken, smothered steak, overstuffed po' boys and muffalettas, gumbo, hot-water cornbread, jambalaya, and boudin are as noteworthy as the giants. Bourbon Street, Mardi Gras, Jackson Square, the French Quarter, and Jazz Fest have attracted tourists by the millions.

The world got a new look at New Orleans when the levees were breached as a result of Katrina, and much of this Southern treasure was underwater—flooded. What the world saw on television screens were thousands of black Americans who lived in such severe poverty, without money or cars, that they were unable to get away before Katrina hit. The scene was not the joyous crowds of fun-seekers slurping fat drinks on Bourbon Street. The scene was frightened, desperate, mostly black Americans whose homes and belongings were lost except for the clothes on their backs and the few things they could carry.

The world saw people pleading for food and water, floating corpses, and throngs of young and old clinging to rooftops to try to escape the rising water in this supposed land of plenty. Federal and state responses were inept. Louisiana State University poet and essayist Andrei Codrescu (2005) writes:

> New Orleans is divided by class, race, and neighborhood. The classes are the rich and the poor. The rich are for the most part white and live uptown and in the French Quarter; the poor are mostly black and live everywhere else. . . . Katrina ripped the veneer off the tourism bureau image of New Orleans like a tin roof. . . . Beneath the thin gloss were the huddled masses of the city's poor with all their good and bad. . . . Their schools were abominable, their health care below civilized standards, their houses barely habitable. (22–23)

When Katrina hit, race and class were the markers of who got out and who did not. The people who had no means to escape New Orleans ended up in shelters, in the Superdome, at the Convention Center, and in the streets. These American citizens were as isolated by poverty as they had been by Jim Crow.

The world saw the behind-the-scenes, out-of-sight New Orleanians who serve the food, clean the hotel rooms, and do other hard work for a minimum wage of $5.15 an hour—if that. The world saw up-close the conditions of life for America's huge excluded class—blacks, Hispanics, poor whites, and others who live well below the nation's unrealistic federal poverty level.

Social Class

Different labels have been used to categorize the economically poor group of Americans that is equal to the entire population of Canada (Alter 2005). They live lives of impoverishment and all that it entails. Some journalists and sociologists use the term *underclass* to depict unemployed or minimum-wage families who are trapped in a cycle of intergenerational poverty. The *New Shorter Oxford English Dictionary* (Brown 1993) defines *underclass* as "a class of people excluded by poverty and unemployment from any opportunity offered by society." The *Encarta World English Dictionary* (Soukhanov 1999) similarly states, "a social class consisting of people so underprivileged that they are seen as being excluded from mainstream society." Other sociologists avoid the word *underclass*. They see it as a pejorative label that puts the blame on individuals for their misfortunes. In his book, *Class and Schools*, Rothstein (2004, 3) uses the term "lower class" for "families of children whose achievement will, on average, be predictably lower than the achievement of middle-class children" because of a variety of economic, health, psychological, and occupational factors. Sered and Fernandopulle (2005) preferred the term *lower caste* to describe individuals who are trapped in a cycle of marginal employment, poor health, and restricted mobility. They characterize the *lower caste* as the new American "untouchable caste" akin to the Hindu pariahs. Sered and Fernandopulle contend, "The current American system in which health care is linked to employment is creating a caste of the chronically ill, infirm, and marginally employed" (15). They intentionally chose the word *caste* for its shock value in describing the plights of impoverished Americans.

Any American town, city, or rural area has a hidden—or at least an ignored—economically poor population. They are the citizens who are excluded from much of what most Americans take for granted: food and water, adequate housing, a decent education, a job with some benefits, an automobile, and a little extra pocket money. Harrington (1962, 3) wrote that America's poor often live "off the beaten track." Poor neighborhoods are not work or travel destinations for most middle- and upper-class individuals. Harrington also commented that the poor are "the wrong age to be seen" (5). Some are old and confined to single rooms due to illness; others are children who are too young to go to school or who do not venture outside their immediate environs. Harrington states, "It is one of the cruelest ironies of social life in advanced countries that the dispossessed at the bottom of society are unable to speak for themselves" (6). It appears that few people want to talk about America's excluded class. They hold no political power and seem to be an embarrassment or nuisance to mainstream society.

The poor and the hungry are found in every part of the nation. For example, America's Second Harvest of Wisconsin found that there are 1,100 food pantries, soup kitchens, and meal programs in the 36 counties of eastern Wisconsin (*Milwaukee Journal Sentinel* 2006). Half of the 235,000 people who rely on Second Harvest for food have household incomes below $10,000 and thus live in extreme poverty. Eleven percent of those who rely on Second Harvest reported that they receive no income at all.

We prefer not to use labels of any type, but for the sake of description, we use the term *excluded class* to describe those Americans who, because of their poverty, the racial and class discrimination they face, and their limited educational opportunities, are excluded from most of what America offers its better-off citizens. In *Class Matters* (2005), *New York Times* correspondents identified four levels of social class in America: lower, working, middle, and upper. We add two additional classes to this hierarchy: the excluded class on the bottom, and the ultra rich on the top. We define the excluded class as the financially poorest American citizens who are trapped in urban and rural enclaves of dilapidated housing, violent neighborhoods, substandard or no medical facilities, crumbling schools with rapid teacher turnover. Many are single-parent families. Some are homeless. They have no safety nets.

The ultra rich (2.7 million people) comprise the top 1 percent of the population that has after-tax income equal to the bottom 100 million U.S. citizens. They are the top 1 percent that owns 47 percent of the wealth of the entire nation (Rank 2004). The ultra rich own multiple trophy-residences in different parts of the country or abroad and penthouses in luxury buildings in major cities. They are the Americans who have private jets and mega-yachts—yachts 200 to 400 feet long that can cost as much as $200 million (Higgins 2006). They are the Americans with easy access to the best health care in the world. Their children have abundant privileges that only money and connections can buy.

Social class structure in America is real and one's social class affects every aspect of one's life. Four elements contribute to one's class status: level of education, income, occupation, and accumulated wealth. The American dream of home ownership and a steady job never has been a reality for many citizens. The long-standing belief was that hard work paid off, and even a child of poverty could rise in social class and become wealthy. Except in rare cases, it hasn't happened that way. Children born to well-educated parents with good incomes, professional occupations, and substantial accumulated or inherited wealth have countless real-life advantages over children born into families with limited education, poverty-level incomes, unemployment or minimum wage employment, and no accumulated wealth.

Although some members of the ultra rich have worked hard for their riches, it is estimated that 80 percent of family wealth derives from the transfer of money from one generation to another—inheritance—rather than from saving employment earnings (Shapiro 2004). The amount of money available for inheritance is related to a family's net worth. In recent years, the median net worth of white families was $198,700 compared to $47,000 for black families. Shapiro states, "Studies indicate that nearly one in four white families (.244) received an inheritance after the death of a parent, averaging $144,652. In stark contrast, about 1 in 20 African American families had inherited in this way, and their average inheritance amounted to $41,985" (67).

Families that inherit money are more likely to own their own homes, among other things, than those who do not receive an inheritance.

Children who come from more privileged backgrounds tend to exhibit more self-assurance in the way they deal with life and have more confidence about future prospects. For example, one of our Long Island interviewees, 13-year-old Nathan, offered the following response to the question, "Do you plan to go to college?" Nathan answered: "I am going to go to college; there has never been any other option for me. I have a lot of ambitions in life, and what I want to do with my life requires a college education. I do not know the exact college that I want to go to, but the college will be a prestigious one. I want to do something with business and law, the exact field I do not know, but my career will be in the realm of business and law."

The children of highly literate parents tend to read better than children of the excluded class because the more fortunate children's parents read and listen to them and ask questions that go beyond factual information. The privileged children expand their vocabularies through more frequent and more complex conversations with adults. In our years of teaching, we have noticed dramatic differences in the vocabularies of children of affluence and children of poverty. With a smaller vocabulary, the chances of comprehending a passage, including a test passage, diminish. If the child does not know the words, the child cannot understand the passage.

Children from the excluded class often do not have anyone at home to help them with homework. We have taught students where the only adults at home were barely functionally literate. Even if the parents had been literate, the home environments were frequently noisy and crowded. Some children could not study in the evenings after dark because the electricity had been turned off due to unpaid bills.

There generally are fewer library books available to poor and minority children. An alternative high school in Brooklyn that serves 200 students has no school library, and there are no textbooks. Rothstein (2004) cites a Philadelphia public library survey that revealed that in wealthy neighborhoods there were "six times as many juvenile" books than in public libraries in black neighborhoods. Furthermore, retail stores stocked "1,300 children's books per 100 children" in college-educated neighborhoods versus "10 books per 100 children" in a multiethnic neighborhood and "fewer than one book per 100 children" in a black neighborhood (58). Rothstein argues:

> Children who are raised by parents who are professionals will, on average, have more inquisitive attitudes toward the material presented by teachers than will children who are raised by working-class parents. As a result, no matter how competent the teacher, the academic achievement of lower-class children will, on average, almost inevitably be less than that of middle-class children. The probability of this reduced achievement increases as the characteristics of lower-socio-class [i.e., the excluded class] families accumulate. (2)

It takes a remarkable human being to overcome all of the obstacles that a child from the excluded class encounters.

Poverty

When Franklin D. Roosevelt became president of the United States in January, 1933, a flurry of important legislation was passed that was directed at addressing the needs of older Americans (the Social Security Act), the rights of workers to unionize (the Wagner Act), unemployment (the Works Progress Administration), and wages (the Fair Labor Standards Act). Historians refer to these acts as The New Deal. In his second inaugural address in January, 1937, Roosevelt described "one-third of a nation ill-housed, ill-clad, ill-nourished . . . tens of millions . . . who at this very moment are denied the greater part of what the very lowest standards of today call the necessities of life" (Keyssar 2005, B7). Alexander Keyssar, a Harvard historian, writes, "The poverty of millions of Americans was viewed as a collective responsibility rather than an assembly of individual misfortunes or failures" (B7). Perhaps that was because during the Great Depression, more of our neighborhoods were poor; poverty was no longer hidden and could no longer be brushed aside.

President Lyndon Johnson, in 1964, launched the Great Society declaring an "unconditional war on poverty" with a goal of eliminating poverty entirely. With the help of various government programs, under the direction of the Office of Economic Opportunity, the official figures on Americans living in poverty dropped from 22 percent in 1959 to 11 percent in 1973 when Richard Nixon became president. A decade later, however, President Ronald Reagan quipped, "The United States declared a war on poverty, and poverty won" (Keyssar 2005, B8). During the George W. Bush years up to 2005, the number of Americans living in poverty had increased to 37 million (Alter 2005).

The Social Security Administration devised a formula to establish poverty levels of income based on minimum needs of families of varying sizes. This formula was introduced at the time of President Lyndon Johnson's War on Poverty. Each year the poverty levels are adjusted to reflect inflation. Entire household gross income before taxes or Social Security deductions is the income figure used. The poverty levels do not take into account differences in the cost of living in different sections of the country or in different states and cities. They do not take into account age, home ownership, or health status. A family with serious medical disabilities living in a rental unit in the New York City borough of Queens will have much higher financial demands than a healthy family with a small house and a large, productive garden in rural Iowa.

The poverty line for a single person is $9,570 per year. The poverty line ranges from $12,830 for two people to $19,350 for four people and $25,870 for six people in the 48 contiguous states and the District of Columbia (U.S. Department of Health and Human Services 2005). Separate, somewhat higher guidelines exist for Alaska and Hawaii where the cost of living is presumed to be more. The Health and Human Services poverty guidelines are slightly different from the poverty thresholds established annually by the Census Bureau. Every thinking person knows that the poverty income cut-offs are unreasonably low for many regions of the country. What family of four could live on $19,350 dollars a year in any of our nation's largest cities or high-cost-of-living coastal areas?

The National Center for Children in Poverty (NCCP) defines *child poverty* as "children who live in families with income below the federal poverty level [FPL]," and "*extreme* child poverty is defined as children who live in families with incomes below half the FPL. Half the annual FPL is $8,045 for a family of three and $9,675 for a family of four" (NCCP 2005, 2). How can any family exist on such a pittance of an annual income? Yet millions of families do. Of the nine states with the highest rates of extreme child poverty, Louisiana ranks first with 13.3 percent of its children living in extreme poverty topped only by the District of Columbia with 19.2 percent. These statistics alone should prod states and districts to transfer money from high-stakes-testing pots to sincere attempts to eradicate child poverty. The NCCP estimates that it actually takes income of at least twice the FPL to meet a family's basic needs. Head Start, the preschool program established in 1965 to combat the effects of poverty, is unavailable to any family of four that earns $20,000 or more annually. What family of four could live on $20,000 on Long Island, New York, where the cost of living is 40 percent higher than the national average? (Long Island Head Start n.d.)

Educators use eligibility for free and reduced lunch as an indicator of poverty. Free lunch is available to children whose family incomes are below 130 percent of the federal poverty level. Reduced lunch is available when families earn no more than 185 percent of that level. Viadero (2006, 15) reports that "researchers and federal statisticians are experimenting with alternative ways to measure the level of poverty in a school or the neighborhoods surrounding it. The search for alternatives stems from concerns about the accuracy of using student eligibility for the federal subsidized-lunch program as a proxy for poverty." The statisticians are considering factors such as resources in the home, social isolation, and "geocoding" geographic identifiers of poverty. This statistical maneuvering and nitpicking surely will result in more children not getting enough to eat.

The Associated Press (2006) announced that 35 million Americans are no longer suffering from hunger. They now are experiencing *food insecurity*. After the 2006 Congressional election, the U.S. Department of Agriculture and the George W. Bush administration replaced the word *hunger* with the euphemistic *food insecurity*. David Beckmann, president of Bread for the World, an antihunger group said that using the euphemism "is a huge disservice to the millions of Americans who struggle daily to feed themselves and their families. We should not hide the word hunger in our discussions of this problem, because we cannot hide the reality of hunger among our citizens." Our government should be addressing the problem of hunger—not camouflaging it.

The patterns of poverty and privilege can be found in every state in the nation. Each state has an excluded class, an ultra-rich class, and all the gradients between. The 2000 Census identified 800,648 Louisianians living below the poverty level (Wilson 2004). Parishes (i.e., counties) in the Mississippi Delta region of Louisiana are collectively the hardest hit with poverty percentages as high as 39.9 percent. Most of the remaining 60 percent of residents of East Carroll, Tensas, and Madison parishes have incomes only slightly above the poverty level. Lake Providence in East Carroll Parish has been called the poorest town in America (White 1997). A former mayor remarked, "We've got all the problems they have in New York City and Chicago, but nothing to fight them with. . . . We've still got a lot of people working in the white folks' kitchens or driving tractors. . . . They're afraid of losing their jobs. They still have to say, 'Yassir, whatever you say'". A young resident of Lake Providence said, "I'd rather shoot myself than stay here. It would be a wasted life." The main street of Lake Providence, with its boarded-up and burned-out buildings looks like a war zone. An exception is the Ole Dutch Bakery that still makes the best lemon poppy seed bread in America ($4.29 a loaf and worth every penny).

A report issued in 2004 (Sumrall) found that 26,327 Louisiana housing units lacked plumbing facilities and 31,797 lacked complete kitchen facilities. Other prevailing housing problems included no indoor toilets, no indoor hot or cold water, bad electrical wiring, and sagging walls with no doors. *Memphis Habitat* (2006) reports that in Memphis, "more than 2,000 local households lack kitchen or plumbing facilities."

Urban poverty is not as hidden as rural poverty due to the sheer number of people who encounter it daily. A train ride past the South Bronx or through sections of Queens or Brooklyn affords the passengers scene after scene of crushing poverty. Lorraine Severson, a teacher in a mostly minority New York public school described the plight of one of her students:

> One of my students lived in a house that burned down—four houses had burned to the ground this fall. He was absent for almost three weeks, and when he showed up one day, he still smelled and looked like he had been in a fire. When I asked where he had been for three weeks, he said he had been in Brooklyn with an aunt. His family doesn't have a car. . . . They don't have any savings. . . . I haven't mentioned the worst aspect of this. My student is diabetic and he went all that time with no insulin—eating when food was available, going in and out

of safe blood levels. If your house burns down, or if your caregiver or sibling dies, or you are seriously ill, you should be exempt from all state tests that year. The fact that the child is still breathing should be evidence enough that life standards have been met.

Doesn't it bother powerbrokers that children in this country do not have flush toilets or running water or even a home while billions of dollars are being spent drilling pupils for standardized tests that may not have any transferability to other learning tasks?

Jackson (2004, 1), in an article titled, "The Third World Next Door," states, "While the stereotype of poverty might be one of dishonest, lazy creatures who abuse welfare and other charitable options, a truer face is one of minimum-wage earners, people working extra jobs and overtime to make ends meet." The view that people who live in poverty do so because of their laziness or other personal faults is held by some Americans—even the young—and especially the privileged. We surveyed young people on Long Island, New York, about a number of issues related to "haves" and "have nots." Long Island is, in many ways, a microcosm of our nation. Nearly 3 million people populate Suffolk and Nassau counties. The number climbs to 7 million when the boroughs of Queens and Brooklyn are added. Our respondents were asked, "Why are people poor? What are the causes of poverty?" Responses from middle- and upper-class students include:

Jake, seventh grader: Because they make poor decisions. They often come from bad families or broken homes. A lot of the time they are lazy.

Samantha, fifth grader: People are poor because they don't work hard enough to make money.

Valerie, sixth grader: Because they don't work hard.

Chase, eighth grader: There is a lot of poverty in the world, and I strongly believe that the main reason is that people do not work hard enough, they are lazy and do not have the motivation to better themselves.

Lynn, tenth grader: Because they are too lazy to get off their butts and get a job. . . . They caused it because if they really cared about being poor, then they would get a job.

Summer, eighth grader: I believe people are poor because of laziness.

Why would well-educated young people in grades five through ten hold such views? Are they recitations of what they hear at home or in school? Are they the opinions of their peers? Do they reflect their sheltered lives? None of our respondents gave any indication that the causes of poverty might include being born into poverty, having no health insurance and large medical bills, inadequate schooling, discrimination in housing and hiring, denied economic opportunities, rent gouging, or federal and state government bureaucracies that do not seem to care enough. Are these topics not discussed by families or in school social studies classes? Have high-stakes testing mandates in reading and math rendered such areas of study "unimportant" or "fluff"?

Racism and Racial Segregation

ERASE Racism, established in 2004, is a Long Island not-for-profit organization devoted to developing and promoting initiatives and policies to end institutional and structural racism. It targets racism in health care, housing, and public education. The group's board of directors includes lawyers, educators, corporate executives, and volunteer organization leaders. Long Island has been identified as "the nation's most segregated suburban area" (Toy, 2004). There are 125 school districts on Long Island, and 76 of them are 80 percent or more white. Forty-four schools are more than 90 percent white. In contrast, the majority of African American and Hispanic students attend schools in just 13 school districts. Seven of the districts have minority enrollments of more than 90 percent (ERASE Racism 2005).

ERASE Racism has differentiated *racial prejudice* and *institutional racism:* "Racial prejudice is an attitude, opinion or feeling, which is usually negative. It is a prejudgment based on myth, missing information, misinformation (lies), or stereotypes about people of color or white people." The organization defines institutional racism as:

> the way government and other public and private institutions systematically afford White people an array of social, political and economic advantages, simply because they are White, while marginalizing and putting at a disadvantage African Americans and many other people of color. . . . Institutional racism is a legacy of American slavery and White settlers' determination to systematically exclude Africans from every aspect of the newly formed democratic society.

As shown in chapter 2, institutional racism has an historical foundation beginning in 1619 and continuing through today—nearly 400 years of racism and racial discrimination in this nation.

Loewen's (2005) *Sundown Towns* provided documentation of a policy of residential racial segregation that flourished in the United States between 1890 and 1940. The legacy of "sundown town" policies remains with us today as can be seen by the number of all-white or nearly all-white towns and cities in most states. Loewen defines a sundown town as "any organized jurisdiction that for decades kept African Americans or other groups from living in it and was thus 'all-white' on purpose" (4). These towns were called sundown towns because through local ordinances, posted warnings, or violence, black Americans were prohibited from being in town after dark or owning or renting property in the town.

Loewen cites a 1922 news story caption in the *Chicago Defender* with a Norman, Oklahoma, dateline that warned, "Don't let the sun set on you here, understand?" (276–277). Loewen's portfolio includes a 1935 linoleum cut depicting a large sign in front of a gallows. The sign stated, "Niggers! Don't let the sun set on you in this town." Another illustration designed by writer Kurt Vonnegut depicts signs from sundown towns surrounding Indianapolis where he grew up. One sign, painted on a board fence said, "Nigger! This is Shepardstown. God help you if the sun ever sets on you here!"

Sundown towns increased during the Jim Crow era as racial discrimination grew. Loewen identifies thousands of sundown towns. They are found in all states but many are in the Midwest. Sizes range from small (e.g., De Land, Illinois, population 470, 2000 U.S. Census) to good-sized (e.g., Appleton, Wisconsin, population 70,087, 2000 U.S. Census). Sundown towns were the forerunners to sundown subdivisions and sundown suburbs. They became more plentiful throughout the last half-century, and the 2000 Census reveals many sundown towns without a single black household. Loewen contends that most towns that are all-white or nearly all-white today remain so from earlier days when they actively excluded blacks and other minorities. In 2006, there was only one black individual in DeLand, Illinois, and only 1 percent of Appleton, Wisconsin's population was African American (ePodunk.com 2006). These two communities' current demographics seem to support Loewen's contention.

Mass housing developments multiplied after World War II with the help of government-insured home loans. Levittown, because of the racial policies of Long Island, New York, had a 1960 population of 82,000 residents—all white. It remains primarily white. Long Island is well-known for its racialized housing policies that have included:

> the use of racially restrictive covenants (agreements among White homeowners that they would not sell their property to Black families), exclusionary zoning (the establishment of minimum zoning requirements that preclude the development of housing that is affordable and desirable to Black families), and real estate practices such as the steering of Blacks into Black neighborhoods and blockbusting (through which realtors induced the panic selling of White-owned homes by fueling fears of neighborhood "takeover"). (ERASE Racism 2005)

Other practices included *redlining* that undervalued neighborhoods that were multiracial, populated primarily by people of color, or that were predicted to experience a "racial transformation." Thomas M. Shapiro, Pokross Chair of Law and Social Policy at Brandeis University, offers this definition of *redlining*:

> Racial redlining encompasses declining to lend in minority neighborhoods, discouraging mortgage loan applications from minority areas, and marketing policies that exclude such areas. Racial redlining reduces housing finance options for borrowers in minority neighborhoods and weakens competition in the mortgage market, which often results in higher mortgage costs and less favorable loan terms. (Shapiro 2004, 108)

Shapiro provides evidence that home ownership by blacks is 25 percent less than for whites [48 percent versus 75 percent]. He cites a Federal Reserve Board study that demonstrated that "lending institutions rejected blacks for home loans 80 percent more often than equally qualified white families" (110).

One of our interviewees, an African American educator, related her exchange with a Long Island realtor:

> I remember vividly stopping in a realtor's office. He ignored me and my husband a few moments and shuffled through papers. Finally he said, "What can I do for you folks today?" We explained that we were interested in knowing more about the community and would like to look at some of the homes. He replied, "You two, most likely, would be better off looking in another community for a home since you cannot afford to live in this area."

Gina Sarducci, a Long Island teacher, told about the housing experience of an acquaintance:

> My mother's friend was trying to build a house in Huntington. She has an Italian last name. The people she was working with had never met her in person, and the paperwork was almost complete. Before the closing on the land, this woman went to see the realtor. A week later, the site in Huntington had fallen through, but she was told there was another site in Riverhead for the same price. This would mean little except that this woman obviously is Puerto Rican. In her Riverhead housing development, almost all of her neighbors are minorities. It seemed to me five years ago when this happened that my mother's Hispanic-looking friend had been moved to the back of the bus, so to speak, as she was given the choice of no house in a largely white community or a house in a poorly funded [largely minority] school district. I wonder if people aren't purposely sending minority children into underfunded districts.

In a number of Long Island communities where home prices are among the highest in the nation, immigrants, mostly Hispanic, are being crammed into substandard housing (Peddie and Laiken 2005). Authorities in Farmingdale found 64 men living in one house. Twelve men living in a basement flooded with sewage were found in a Westbury house. Immigrants have been living in sheds without heat or water in Southampton Village, and in Huntington Station, men had to climb through a hole in the wall to reach their sleeping cubbyholes. A five-bedroom home in North Hempstead was converted to nine bedrooms and rented to 30 tenants who paid $250 each per month—a total rent of $7,500 a month and $90,000 a year. A North Hempstead supervisor said, "There's a whole world that people are living in, this life that no one knows about and no one wants to know about" (A2).

Lambert (2005) reports on a survey that showed that "a majority of Long Islanders—56 percent—say that they may move away within five years" (B5). Soaring housing prices, heavy tax burdens, and the overall cost of living are driving them out. In some neighborhoods, as residents move out, speculators buy their old homes and pack them with mostly minority persons. It is not unusual to see 10 or 15 automobiles parked outside a moderate-sized house on Long Island.

Old, run-down, two- or three-bedroom, one-bathroom houses built in the 1940s and 1950s routinely sell for $400,000 to $700,000 on Long Island. The median home price in 2006 for Nassau County was $485,000 and for Suffolk County was $390,000 (Lambert 2005, B5). Executive homes and estates range from $1.5 million to $20 million or more. In Sotheby's (2005) Long Island housing listing, there are 22 homes ranging from $3,200,000 to $23,500,000. Gaines (2006) describes a 20,000 square foot home in Bridgehampton, Long Island, with its own 18-hole golf course, a 75-foot swimming pool, and a guest house; the property is listed for $75 million. Chester Hartman (2006), research director of the Poverty and Race Research Action Council notes, "Housing is fast becoming the most obvious symbol and manifestation of the nation's obscene and growing gap between the super-rich and the rest of us" (A22). We realize that some Hamptons folks earned every penny; others inherited large sums. But children from the trailer parks and those from the estates are required to take the same high-stakes tests in New York if they attend public schools. The comparative outcome is a foregone conclusion.

Social Class Segregation

If one takes a drive through the expanding suburbs west and north of Chicago, one will see new housing developments advertised within a specific price range such as "Exclusive homes: $325,000 to $395,000." A few miles down the road, billboards announce "Executive homes from $395,000 to $449,000." This trend is described in *Suburban Nation* (Duany, Plater-Zyberk, and Speck 2000). Subdivisions are segregated on the basis of small gradations of income or the ability to afford mortgage payments. Real estate agents tout the ZIP codes, the impressive addresses, the local school high-stakes test scores, and other features. To what extent is this type of economic segregation a marker of racial segregation? Numerous subdivisions nationwide have formed homeowners' associations. The associations devise rules and regulations designed to protect property values through covenants and agreements that keep "undesirable types" from settling in the subdivision. According to Loewen (2005), "One of the first neighborhood associations, the University District Property Owners' Association near Los Angeles, was established in 1922 as the Anti-African Housing Association" (391). Price restrictions, exclusivity, covenants, and regulations may mask an insidious form of racial and social class segregation.

Gated communities are the most recent extension of homeowner associations and economically segregated subdivisions. These communities purportedly are designed to provide security and protection from crime. Gated communities typically adjoin a golf course, a marina, or a winter ski area. Loewen (2005) estimates that about 3 million American households were in gated communities by 1997. In the decade since then, that number has expanded enormously. Loewen cites a Maryland realtor who said, "Any upscale community now would have to be gated. That's what makes it upscale" (392). The gates and gatehouses in many such communities are largely symbolic, rarely staffed, and serve no security function.

Just outside Monroe, Louisiana, is an exclusive subdivision called Frenchman's Bend. Many of its large homes front on an 18-hole golf course or face a meandering bayou. One enters Frenchman's Bend by approaching a gatehouse with security cameras and then drives past imposing, lushly landscaped brick homes. The clubhouse hosts a first-class restaurant, meeting rooms for social events, and a pro shop. A large in-ground pool with deck chairs and lounging areas complete the grounds. In the clubhouse, children can "run a tab" billed to their parents' membership accounts. The golf course has a paved pathway for golf carts throughout its 18 well-manicured greens and fairways. Every homeowner is automatically and necessarily a member of the Frenchman's Bend Homeowners Association, Inc., a nonprofit corporation. Each home owner is assessed an annual fee. The Association is governed by an elected Board of Directors who are empowered to make "reasonable rules and regulations" governing matters of the subdivision (Parish of Ouachita 1992, 6).

Gated communities hold appeal for those who can afford "exclusive" living, and increasingly, they appeal to retirees who have accumulated wealth or retirement accounts that enable them to purchase homes in these sheltered environments. "Exclusive" neighborhoods and communities, by definition, leave out the millions of Americans in the excluded and lower classes. Segregation by socioeconomics assures that most gated communities are "overwhelmingly white, although race goes unmentioned" (Loewen 2005, 392).

Advantages of Wealth

Bountiful amenities are available to the upper class and the ultra rich and their children. Included are special schools that cater to children with some form of learning disabilities. Tuition costs are beyond the means of the working class, the lower class, or the excluded class. Private schools in New York City with programs for students who have learning difficulties include The Churchill School (tuition $27,000 per year), Robert Louis Stevenson School (tuition $28,000 per year), Winston Preparatory School (tuition $31,950 per year), York Preparatory School (tuition $23,000 per year plus $9,800 for Jump Start), and Columbia Grammar and Preparatory School ($44,000 per year for the LD Track) (Blau 2003, 34). These are 2003 tuition costs; the poverty level for a family of four in 2005 was $19,350 per year.

Education Unlimited offers a 10-day College Admission Prep Camp at Tufts University. The cost is $2,250. The Camp provides 28 hours of SAT preparation to help its enrollees become admissible to good colleges (Tonn 2005). A mother explained why she sent her daughter to the Tufts camp. Her daughter is a student at a private boarding school in New Jersey: "Getting into college has become so competitive, one has to give their child every tool possible" (35). How can members of the working, lower, and excluded classes compete with these fortunate children on the same SAT test? How can so many colleges rely on SAT scores when they know about the special tutoring advantages available to the affluent but not to the impoverished?

Princeton Review, a testing and test preparation corporation, runs a SAT preparation program at a beach house in the Hamptons on Long Island. The cost of the program is $7,500 (Marks 2005). Brendan Mernin is one of the SAT tutors charging "upwards of $300 an hour to increase the admissions chances of the area's princelings" (14). On one occasion, Mr. Mernin tutored a teenage girl twice a week on the family yacht.

Boston University Academy advertises itself as "an excellent high school that comes complete with its own university" (Boston University Academy 2002, 51). The small school charged nearly $23,000 in tuition and fees for the 2005–2006 school year and had an enrollment of 156 students (Boston University Academy 2006). The school features a classical approach including Greek and Latin, challenging academics, and an advanced placement program that enables students to earn up to 48 college credits by the time they graduate from 12th grade. Boston University Academy has produced Rhodes scholars, students who have published in international journals, actors, symphony musicians, and members of the robotics teams of the Boston University College of Engineering. Academy students may participate in activities such as fencing, squash, sailing, crew, martial arts, ballroom dancing, and more.

All of the foregoing are advantages that the youth of the excluded class could only dream about if they even knew such riches existed. One of our former graduate students taught mostly black junior high school students in a midsized city in Louisiana. Competing basketball teams did not want to play in the school's gymnasium because of the deplorable conditions of the facility's locker rooms and court. Our student had to take his team's uniforms home after each game and wash them because each player had only one uniform and many had no modern way of laundering their uniforms at home. This was the job of the teacher-coach who felt fortunate to have a washing machine in his apartment building. The deck is stacked against these junior high students and others like them who have so many disadvantages at home and at school. In the following chapter, the relationships among poverty, health and dental care, and schooling are examined, and we will see more evidence of a stacked deck.

References

Alter, J. 2005. The other America. *Newsweek*, September 19, 42–48.

Associated Press. 2006. 35M in U.S. had "food insecurity" in 2005. *CBS News*, November 15. www.cbsnews.com (accessed November 21, 2006).

Blau, M. 2003. Learning curve. *New York*, June 9, 31–35, 79.

Boston University Academy. 2002. Boston University Academy is an excellent high school that comes complete with its own university. *New York Times*, December 15, 51.

———. 2006. Boston University Academy. www.buacademy.org (accessed January 7, 2006).

Brown, L., ed. 1993. *New shorter Oxford English dictionary*. Oxford, UK: Oxford University Press.

Codrescu, A. 2005. City of ghosts. *National Geographic special edition on Katrina*, December 26, 2005, 22–23.

Correspondents of *The New York Times*. 2005. *Class matters*. New York: Henry Holt and Company.

Duany, A., E. Plater-Zyberk, and J. Speck. 2000. *Suburban nation*. New York: Farrar, Straus, and Giroux.

ePodunk.com. 2006. Appleton (WI) community profile, De Land (IL) community profile. www.epodunk.com (accessed July 11, 2006).

ERASE Racism. 2005. *Brown v. Board of Education*: The unfinished agenda conference monograph. www.eraseracismny.org/downloads/speeches_presentations/ ERASE_Monograph2005.pdf (accessed April 20, 2005).

Gaines, S. 2006. Hamptons holdouts. *New York*, June 26, 64–69.

Harrington, M. 1962. *The other America: Poverty in the United States*. New York: Simon & Schuster, 1993.

Hartman, C. 2006. Big houses, no homes. *New York Times*, letter to the editor, March 20.

Higgins, M. 2006. The new megayachts: Too much of a good thing? *New York Times*, January 13, D1, D5.

Jackson, T. P. 2004. The third world next door. *Monroe (LA) News Star*, December 5. www.thenewsstar.com/localnews/html (accessed December 5, 2004).

Keyssar, A. 2005. Reminders of poverty, soon forgotten. *The Chronicle Review*, November 4, B6–B8.

Lambert, B. 2005. More Long Islanders want to go, poll finds. *New York Times*, December 1, B5.

Loewen, J. W. 2005. *Sundown towns: A hidden dimension of American racism*. New York: New Press.

Long Island Head Start. n.d. No one should be left out. *Long Island Head Start* (brochure).

Marks, A. 2005. SAT beach house. *New York*, August 15, 14.

Memphis Habitat. 2006. A profile of poverty housing in the United States and Memphis. Habitat for Humanity of Greater Memphis. www.memphishabitat.com (accessed March 2, 2006).

Milwaukee Journal Sentinel. 2006. Hunger still stalks Wisconsin. June 8, 18A.

National Center for Children in Poverty. 2005. Who are America's poor children? www.nccp.org/pub_cpt05b.html (accessed December 6, 2005).

Parish of Ouachita. 1992. *Declaration of covenants and restrictions affecting Frenchman's Bend subdivision*. September 9, Sterlington, LA.

Peddie, S., and E. Laikin. 2005. Crowds of illegal homes. *Newsday*, July 15, A2–A3.

Rank, M. R. 2004. *One nation, underprivileged: Why American poverty affects us all*. Oxford, UK: Oxford University Press.

Rothstein, R. 2004. *Class and schools: Using social, economic, and educational reform to close the black-white achievement gap*. New York: Teachers College Columbia University and Washington, DC: Economic Policy Institute.

Shapiro, T. M. 2004. *The hidden cost of being African American*. Oxford, UK: Oxford University Press.

Sered, S. S., and R. Fernandopulle. 2005. *Uninsured in America: Life and death in the land of opportunity*. Berkeley, CA: University of California Press.

Soukhanov, A. H. 1999. *Encarta World English Dictionary*. New York: St. Martin's Press.

Sotheby's. 2005. For the ongoing collection of life. Sotheby's International Realty, 18–24 (brochure).

Sumrall, B. 2004. Pineville housing program to provide "fresh start." *Alexandria (LA) Town Talk*, December 10. www.thetowntalk.com/html (accessed December 10, 2004).

Tonn, J. L. 2005. A leg up. *Education Week*, August 10, 35–37.

Toy, V. 2004. Open arms, closed doors and racism. Wired New York. February 22. www.wirednewyork.com/forum/ (accessed January 15, 2006).

U. S. Department of Health and Human Services. 2005. The 2005 HHS poverty guidelines. aspe.hhs.gov/poverty/05poverty.shtml (accessed November 20, 2005).

Viadero, D. 2006. Scholars test out new yardsticks of school poverty. *Education Week*, November 8, 1, 15.

White, J. E. 1997. The poorest place in America. www.geocities.com/BourbonStreet/
      3754/timearticle.html (accessed January 7, 2006). (Originally from the August 15, 1997
      edition of *Time* magazine.)

Wilson, L. 2004. "I want to get out." *Monroe (LA) News-Star.* November 14. www
      .thenewsstar.com (accessed November 14, 2004).

4

Health Issues

M ARK ROBERT RANK (2004), PROFESSOR OF SOCIAL WELFARE at Washington University, observes, "One of the most consistent findings in epidemiology is that the quality of an individual's health is negatively affected by lower socioeconomic status, particularly impoverishment." Rank's review of literature reveals a number of serious health risks associated with poverty including, "heart disease, diabetes, hypertension, cancer, infant mortality, mental illness, undernutrition, lead poisoning, asthma, and dental problems" (39). One of the cruelties of the school accountability movement and its high-stakes tests is the disregard of children's basic health needs. The judgment of students' achievement based on a single test score without thought given to their home and neighborhood circumstances can be endorsed only by those who have not worked daily and recently with pupils who are in pain because of lack of dental care or are in poor health because of lack of medical care.

Dental Problems

Christopher, a Long Island 12th grader, commented:

I have been working since I was 14 and got my working papers. I worked every summer changing tires, and now I work during the school year because I need to have money to fix my teeth where the enamel broke off. My mom tried to get benefits but was turned down. I hope I get a job that has good benefits so I can see a doctor instead of the clinic all the time and see a dentist instead of the students at

Stony Brook. I mean, they are good, but it scares me that they aren't really dentists yet and they get to practice on my teeth.

A concern about teeth is not a concern unique to Christopher. Sered and Fernandopulle (2005) argue that two physical characteristics often are indicators of membership in the "lower caste"—those Americans who live below the poverty level. The characteristics are rotten teeth and obesity. The researchers describe a young woman in Idaho who covered her mouth during their interview because she was embarrassed about her bad teeth. They write about a man in Mississippi who used pliers to pull out his own decaying teeth. The heartbreaking images of the impoverished blacks in New Orleans who were flooded out by Hurricane Katrina and the breached levees often included children and adults with decayed or missing teeth. In the critical ethnography, *High Stakes: Poverty, Testing, and Failure in American Schools* (2006), Johnson and Johnson describe teaching in an underfunded Louisiana school serving mostly African American children who live in poverty: pupils crying because of painful teeth, finding rotten little teeth on their classroom floor, and learning that only a small percentage of their students ever had been to a dentist.

Dental problems are not just visual indicators of a high-poverty existence. They contribute to other more serious medical conditions including heart disease, diabetes, and obesity. Individuals with rotten, painful teeth must steer clear of many types of nutritious foods such as salads, whole grain foods, fruits, and nuts. Soft foods, processed foods, creamed soups, ice cream, and fast-food take-outs often comprise the diets of the poor.

Fleck (2006, 14) describes the problem: "Marie Burton craves chilled watermelon and other cool fresh fruit, but she can't eat them. Carrot sticks are a favorite, and she adores a thick steak, but she can't eat those, either. Cold, chewy or crunchy cuisine is off-limits for Burton because her teeth hurt too much—at least the ones she has left. They're wiggly, broken and infected." Marie Burton's $22,000-a-year job does not provide her with sufficient insurance to get her teeth fixed. She stays home from social events because of embarrassment. "I don't like looking in the mirror or talking to people unless I have to," she said. Burton is one of 108 million Americans who have no dental insurance.

In many low-income neighborhoods, urban and rural, dental care is not readily available nor is it affordable to the local residents, most of whom have no dental insurance. Medicaid, in most states, does not cover dental needs. Sered and Fernandopulle (2005), who conducted interview research with uninsured Americans, report, "Almost every time we ask interviewees what their first priority would be if the president established universal health coverage tomorrow, the immediate answer was 'my teeth.'"(166).

In 2000, the U.S. Department of Health and Human Services issued *Oral Health in America: A Report of the Surgeon General.* The *Report* states, "What amounts to a 'silent epidemic' of oral diseases is affecting our most vulnerable citizens—poor children, the elderly, and many members of racial and ethnic minority groups" (1). The *Report* pointed out the "striking disparities" between poor children and those who can afford dental care and have dental insurance. Low-income children, for example, have twice the tooth decay as their economically better-off peers. Children without dental insurance are "three times more likely" to have dental problems than children who have dental insurance. These circumstances are even more distressing today. In the first four years of George W. Bush's presidency, the number of poor Americans, most of whom are children, increased by 5.4 million, and the number of uninsured Americans increased by 6 million (Shields 2005).

Most politicians and policymakers ignore the effects of poor dental care on school accountability scores; however even a child knows it is difficult to do one's best work when in pain. The Surgeon General's *Report* reveals: "The social impact of oral diseases in children is substantial. More than 51 million school hours are lost each year to dental-related illness. Poor children suffer nearly 12 times more restricted–activity days than children from higher-income families. Pain and suffering due to untreated [dental] diseases can lead to problems in eating, speaking, and attending to learning" (2).

The *Child Trends Data Bank* (2005, 1) states: "Untreated oral diseases may lead to problems in eating, speaking, and sleeping. Poor oral health among children has been tied to poor performance in school and poor social relationships. Children with chronic dental pain may have difficulty concentrating, poor self-image, and problems completing schoolwork."

Another problem poor families encounter is finding someone to treat them for dental care. Hanford (2005) quotes a 46-year-old mother who said that she never went to a dentist because "the priority is making sure the kids have something to eat. . . . Your teeth only become a priority when you get a toothache" (1). Hanford adds, "But if you're poor and you get a toothache, you may have a very hard time finding a dentist who will treat you" (1). In a report from the American Dental Association, Berthold (2003) notes that access to dentists is difficult even if a child gets help from Medicaid. He suggests that Medicaid's "low reimbursement" to dental offices and "cumbersome administration" for dentists impede the poor's access to care. If a poor family can find a dentist who will treat them, Berthold pointed out that they wait about "40 percent longer for their first appointment than persons with private insurance," and must travel farther to get to a dentist—even though transportation options often are limited to those living in poverty.

Obesity

The second principal marker of socioeconomic status identified by Sered and Fernandopulle is obesity. For many Americans, poverty and obesity go hand-in-hand. Harrington (1962) aptly refers to many poor individuals as being "fat with hunger, for that is what cheap foods do" (2). Diet and fitness cost money and take time—two commodities not readily available to poor women or men working one or more minimum wage jobs to raise their families. The states with the highest proportion of obese people are typically the states with the highest concentration of poverty. Obesity is linked to a number of health problems including diabetes (sometimes resulting in amputation of limbs), high blood pressure (sometimes resulting in strokes), and stress damage to the musculoskeletal system (sometimes resulting in falls, broken bones, and other injuries).

There is a stigma attached to obesity. Obese individuals are given derogatory nicknames and subjected to taunting jingles beginning in childhood. Overweight people are seen to lack self-control and to be gluttonous, self-indulgent, and lazy. Sered and Fernandopulle (2005) report, "Negative feelings toward obesity continue into adulthood . . . studies document discrimination against overweight people in education, rental housing, and . . . employment" (167).

The *New England Journal of Medicine* estimates that the alarming rise in childhood obesity eventually could cut children's life expectancies by as much as five years (Belluck 2005). Dr. David S. Ludwig, Director of the obesity program at Boston Children's Hospital, said: "There is an unprecedented increase in prevalence of obesity at younger and younger ages without much obvious public health impact. But when they start developing heart attack, stroke, kidney failures, amputations, blindness, and ultimately death at younger ages, then that could be a huge effect on life expectancy" (A18).

In a study conducted by the U.S. Department of Education's National Center for Education Statistics, researchers found that "schools in which three-quarters or more of children who are poor get less time for recess than those in more affluent schools" (Viadero 2006, 14). Without physical activity during the school day, children of the excluded class have a better chance of becoming obese than do those from more affluent backgrounds.

School lunch menus in America underscore socioeconomic differences that can sabotage healthy eating for those who are born poor. For example, at the Calhoun School in New York City, where tuition for grades kindergarten through 12 ranges from $23,600-$27,600 per year (Calhoun School 2005), all the chefs are graduates of the French Culinary Institute. The school's website states, "Yogurt and fresh fruit is available every day, along with an extensive salad bar." Items on the lunch menu might include quinoa with sautéed shiitakes, roasted codfish with crisp panko and mustard top, broccoli rabe, salmon and spinach lasagna, and brown basmati rice pilaf. At the Dwight School on New York City's Central Park West, parents can choose menu items for their children. The options include vegetarian selections and "Smart & Fit (Healthy)" items (Dwight School 2005).

In contrast, the Louisiana public school in which two of the authors of this volume taught lists glazed donuts, sausage, rice krispie treat, tater tots, pig 'n flapjacket with syrup, and cinnamon rolls among their menu items (*Homer Guardian-Journal* 2005). The Louisiana school serves mostly African American children who are among the poorest of the poor. They need nutritious food because they often do not get enough to eat at home. Most receive free breakfast and free lunch, and for some of the pupils, these school meals are the only food they get all day. The American Academy of Pediatrics (Block and Krebs 2005) identified insufficient nutrition as the primary cause of children's "failure to thrive" (FTT). The Academy warns, "The fundamental cause of FTT is nutritional deficiency. Poverty is the greatest single risk factor worldwide and in the United States." The Academy adds, "The malnutrition in children in FTT can lead not only to impaired growth but also to long-term deficits in intellectual, social, and psychological functioning."

A recent federal law, the Child Nutrition Act, requires healthier free and reduced breakfasts and lunches in schools that receive federal funds. Time will tell how the law plays out in actual practice because as of this writing, there are no penalties, as there are for low test scores, if the Child Nutrition Act is not followed (Samuels 2006).

State Rankings in Poverty and Health

Each year, Morgan Quitno Press publishes a list of state health rankings on the basis of several factors. Those factors include low birth weight percentages, prenatal care of mothers, infant mortality rate, state health care expenditures, percent of population not covered by health insurance, percent of population lacking access to primary care, beds in community hospitals, and more. The 12 unhealthiest states in American in 2005, according to the Morgan Quitno (2005) rankings, show a dramatic overlap with the 12 states that have the highest percentage of children living in poverty (*Kids Count Data Book 2005*, 2005), the 12 states with the highest percentage of minorities (*Chronicle of Higher Education* 2005), and the 12 states with the lowest fourth-grade reading achievement scores (National Center for Education Statistics 2005). This can be seen in table 4.1.

TABLE 4.1.
State Rankings

Rank	Health	Child Poverty	Minorities	Reading Achievement
39	Arizona	South Carolina	Alabama	Georgia
40	Arkansas	Tennessee	South Carolina	Tennessee
41	Alabama	Arizona	Florida	Oklahoma
42	Georgia	Oklahoma	Georgia	South Carolina
43	South Carolina	Texas	Arizona	Alaska
44	Florida	Alabama	Louisiana	Hawaii
45	Texas	Arkansas	Mississippi	Alabama
46	Oklahoma	Kentucky	New York	Louisiana
47	Nevada	West Virginia	Texas	Arizona
48	New Mexico	New Mexico	California	California
49	Mississippi	Mississippi	New Mexico	New Mexico
50	Louisiana	Louisiana	Hawaii	Mississippi

Six states appear on all four lists: Alabama, Louisiana, Mississippi, South Carolina, Arizona, and New Mexico. Alabama and Mississippi have the highest percentages of obese people in the nation—more than 28 percent of each state's population (Ash 2005). Four of the six states, Alabama, South Carolina, Louisiana, and Mississippi, have the highest percentages of black Americans in the United States. The two Southwestern states, Arizona and New Mexico, have large percentages of Hispanics and Native Americans (*Chronicle of Higher Education* 2005). The overlap among poverty, reading achievement, minority classification, and health is unmistakable.

That these states rank at the bottom in reading achievement (Mississippi) or near the bottom (Louisiana, Alabama, South Carolina) is not surprising. The other unhealthiest states, Arizona, Texas, Oklahoma, Nevada, and New Mexico, have high concentrations of child poverty, high percentages of minorities, and low reading achievement. The pattern is clear. Federal and state education officials' failure to see these connections is inexcusable. Instead of blaming students and teachers for low test scores, punishing them with negative labels, grade repetition, withholding funds, and diminishing their educational experiences with test after test, the federal and state government must address the real issues. They must commit resources to alleviate the serious damages of poverty and poor health. They must initiate corrective justice because the deck is stacked against less privileged children.

The Impact of Social Factors

Richard Wilkinson, professor of social epidemiology at the University of Nottingham, argues that the quality of social relations and low social status are among the most powerful influences on health. Wilkinson's premise is presented at the outset of his work, *The Impact of Inequality* (2005, 1):

> Within each of the developed countries, including the United States, average life expectancy is five, ten, or even fifteen years shorter for people living in the poorest areas compared to those in the richest. . . . During the last few decades the health differences between classes have increased. They reveal such a gulf between the lives and experience of rich and poor, well educated and less well educated, and, through the same social and economic stratification, different racial or ethnic groups, that they call into question the humanity, morality, and values of modern societies.

Wilkinson cites research by Geronimus, Bound, Waidmann, Colen, and Steffick that examined data from 23 rich and poor areas in the United States. The researchers found that white women and white men living in the wealthiest areas could expect to live 16 years longer than black women and black men living in the poorest areas. Death rates in all 23 communities were closely related to median household income. Black Americans living in poverty are deprived of 20 percent to 25 percent of the longevity of whites in the wealthiest communities. Epstein (2003, 75, 79) describes how poverty breeds illnesses in children: "In America's rundown urban neighborhoods, the diseases associated with old age are afflicting the young. . . . You wake up stressed, you go to sleep stressed, you see all the garbage and the dealers. . . .You say, 'What's the use of doing anything?'"

Wilkinson (2005) found that social relations are better in societies in which income differences between wealthy and poor are smaller and the relations are worse where the differences are larger. People are more trusting and have longer life expectancies in states where the income differences are smaller. Using a scale called *The Robin Hood Index of Income Irregularity* (the percentage of a society's income that would need to be taken from the rich and given to the poor to achieve equity), Wilkinson discusses research that revealed the differences in how people trust one another when income differences are greatest. That research showed that the individuals residing in states with the greatest income differences (e.g., Louisiana, Mississippi, Alabama, New York, Texas, and Kentucky) had the greatest amount of mutual distrust. Three of these states also appear on all four lists presented in table 4.1: Louisiana, Mississippi, and Alabama are among the unhealthiest states, have the most African Americans, have the highest percentages of children living in poverty, and have some of the lowest fourth-grade reading scores in the nation.

Research by Harvard political science professor Robert Putnam has shown that social capital, that is, involvement in community life (e.g., voting, belonging to groups, reading local newspapers), also is strongly related to income equality (Wilkinson 2005). The six states with the most unequal incomes also had the lowest levels of social capital. The pattern, therefore, holds. Where there is greater disparity in income levels, there is more mistrust and a greater disconnect within the community. Both contribute to stress and result in poor health.

Wilkinson has illustrated the pathways that lead from income inequality and poverty to ill health. Income inequality and poverty lead to greater social status differences, less trust, and low community involvement. These, in turn, lead to stress, depression, insecurity, aggression, shame, and social anxiety. The end effects of these conditions are ill health, drug and alcohol abuse, antisocial behavior, and violence. This is a cruel cycle that needs to be tackled at its roots, economic and social inequality, if corrective justice is to be achieved. These inequalities hit minorities the hardest. Nearly 25 percent of black Americans and 22 percent of Hispanics live in poverty compared to eight percent of white Americans (Alter 2005). In some counties and parishes in Mississippi, Louisiana, Alabama, Texas, New Mexico, Arizona, Kentucky, and West Virginia, up to 56.9 percent of the population were living in poverty according to the 2000 Census. Most of these counties and parishes also have the highest percentages of minority residents.

Children's Defense Fund Findings

The Children's Defense Fund (2005) periodically issues reports on the state of America's children. The report for 2005 contains some unnerving statistics:

- Twenty-three million adults and thirteen million children live in households suffering from hunger or "food insecurity without hunger."
- More than nine million children have no health insurance.
- Infants born to black mothers are more than twice as likely to die before their first birthday as infants born to white mothers.
- The number of overweight children has more than tripled since 1980. Almost nine million young people are overweight—15.5 percent of all children under age nineteen.

Moments in America for Children (2004), published by the Children's Defense Fund, includes a number of statistics pertaining to African American, Latino, and American Indian children.

African American children:

- Every two minutes a baby is born into poverty.
- Every four minutes a child is born without health insurance.
- Every seven minutes a child is born at low birthweight.
- Every fifteen minutes a baby is born to a mother who received late or no prenatal care.
- Every hour a child dies before her or his first birthday.

Latino children:

- Every two minutes a child is born into poverty.
- Every two minutes a child is born without health insurance.
- Every nine minutes a child is born at low birthweight.
- Every eleven minutes a baby is born to a mother who has received late or no prenatal care.
- Every two hours a child dies before his or her first birthday.

American Indian children:

- Every thirty-six minutes a child is born into poverty.
- Every three hours a child is born to a mother who received late or no prenatal care.
- Every three hours a baby is born at low birthweight.
- Every twenty-two hours a baby dies before his or her first birthday.

The statistics disseminated by the Children's Defense Fund should serve as a call to action for another war on poverty and racial discrimination in this nation that has so much wealth so unevenly distributed. Is such a war likely in a nation with a history of racism among large segments of our population?

Perhaps William J. Bennett, former U.S. Secretary of Education, was not aware of these statistics when he shocked the country with his statement to a radio talk show host. Bennett said, "But I do know, that it's true that if you wanted to reduce crime, if that were your sole purpose, you could abort every black baby in this country and your crime rate would go down" (Brewington 2005). To the degree that such views are held by persons with power or influence, the likelihood of eradicating or even lessening institutional racism decreases.

Kids Count Findings

The problems identified by the Children's Defense Fund are amplified by research conducted by the Annie E. Casey Foundation. The findings are presented yearly in the *Kids Count Data Book* that includes national and state profiles. The 2005 *Kids Count Data Book* (30) contains a comparison of groups on key indicators of child well-being. These indicators include percent of low birthweight babies, infant mortality rate (deaths per 100,000 live births), child death rate (deaths per 100,000 of children ages 1–14), and percent of children living in poverty. Table 4.2 gives the comparisons for whites, African Americans, American Indians, and Latinos.

TABLE 4.2.
Key Indicators of Child Well-Being

Indicator	White	African American	American Indian	Latino
Low birthweight	6.9	13.3	7.2	6.5
Infant mortality	5.8	13.8	8.6	5.6
Child death rate	19	31	28	20
Child poverty	10	34	32	38

The table shows that the groups that fare the worst on these indicators of child well-being are African Americans followed by American Indians and then Latinos. White children, overall, fare the best. The two lowest-ranking states on these four indicators are Louisiana and Mississippi. These two states appear over and over again on the negative side of nearly every type of state ranking. Kristof (2005, 11) reports: "In both Mississippi and Louisiana infant mortality is worse (for every 1,000 babies born, 10 die in their first year of life) than in Costa Rica (8 die per 1,000). For black babies in either state, the picture is still more horrifying: 15 die per 1,000. In poor, war-torn Sri Lanka, where per capita medical spending is only $131, babies have better odds, with 13 dying per 1,000."

The acute problems of high rates of extreme poverty, racial discrimination, un- and underemployment, substandard housing, and run-down school buildings need to be seriously and immediately addressed. Other states of the Deep South and Southwest (see table 4.1) also need societal reconstruction—corrective justice—if the millions of Americans in the excluded class are to be brought into the mainstream.

The Racial Divide

Randall (2005) summarized her review of research related to health and race in the United States and abroad. She demonstrates that *race* is a social construct that has been shaped by cultural, political, and ideological functions. *Race* had not been shown to be determined genetically or biologically. Nonetheless, race has great bearing on health status and health care. Randall concludes:

> Racial barriers to quality health care may manifest themselves in a number of ways: lack of economic access to health care; barriers to hospitals; barriers to physicians and other providers; discriminatory policies and practices . . . disparities in medical treatment. . . . Studies have shown racial disparity in both quality and availability of treatment in AIDS, cardiology, cardiac surgery, kidney disease, organ transplantation, internal medicine, obstetrics, prescription drugs, treatment for mental illness, and hospital care. (4)

Bell and Minaya (2005) report similar findings. There is a significant gap in the medical treatment afforded white and minority patients. They cite a study in *The New England Journal of Medicine* that showed that "black Medicare recipients were less likely to get nine kinds of potentially life-saving or life-altering surgery than whites, even when overall medical needs were the same." Some of the procedures were heart valve replacements, appendectomies, back surgeries, and hip and knee replacements. Black men in Medicare in Baltimore were "63 percent less likely than white counterparts to have heart bypass surgery." Other researchers have found that blacks had fewer angiogram examinations to assess and repair blocked blood vessels. These racial gaps in health care may be attributable to low income, lack of insurance, access to nearby medical care, and discrepancies in the quality of Medicare, but other factors include racism and discrimination against members of the excluded class.

Boutique Doctors

In recent years, a new phenomenon has developed to further separate the medical care of those with money from those without. Zuger (2005) describes the onset of "concierge medicine" with boutique doctors who are on call to those who can afford their retainers. Referred to as a "deluxe model of medicine," those who can pay for this luxury rave about it and state that it costs no more than cruises or other luxuries they enjoy. Annual retainer fees range from $1,500 to $10,000. These fees are in addition to the regular medical costs the patient incurs. Features offered by boutique doctors include same- or next-day appointments; private waiting rooms; home delivery of medication; telephone, e-mail, and pager access to physicians; home consultation; and coordination of medical care when traveling. Critics of boutique doctors accuse the physicians of abandoning patients who cannot pay their retainers, thus creating a two-class system of medicine. Perhaps it actually is a three-class system of medical care: the care received by the boutique patients, the medical care of other mainstream patients with insurance, and the medical care available to members of the excluded class—often emergency rooms or clinics staffed by physician assistants. Rank (2004, 210) sums up the situation: "As with education, access to quality health care is largely dependent upon the size of one's wallet. For those who can afford it, America offers the finest medical care in the world. Those unable to absorb the increasing costs are frequently left out in the cold, without health care."

The United States, unlike most industrialized, technologically advanced nations, has no system of national health care. Health care largely is a for-profit system (profit for insurers, doctors, pharmaceutical companies, medical suppliers, and hospitals) that relies on employer-sponsored health insurance, private health insurance, or personal payment. Those Americans without insurance, unless they are wealthy, spend every day at risk. Leading causes of bankruptcies and homelessness in this nation are insurmountable medical bills that families cannot afford to pay. Herbert (2005, 220–221) articulates his disgust with the medical support system:

> It seems extremely strange that in the United States of America, the richest, most powerful nation in the history of the world, we are going backward in the twenty-first century in our ability to provide the most fundamental kinds of health care to ordinary people, including children. . . . Maybe the nation itself needs a doctor. Shoving low-income people, including children off the health care rolls at a time when the economy is allegedly booming is a sure sign of some kind of sickness in the society.

Herbert's comments stemmed from the release of a report from the Center on Budget Policy Priorities that showed that between 2002 and 2004, 34 states had made large cuts in public health insurance programs including Medicaid. More than half a million children lost coverage.

Krugman (2005) denounced President George W. Bush and the Republican administration for neglect of race issues and poverty. In the weeks just after Hurricane Katrina, Krugman writes:

> The administration's lethally inept response to Hurricane Katrina had a lot to do with race. For race is the biggest reason the United States, uniquely among advanced countries, is ruled by a political movement that is hostile to the idea of helping citizens in need. . . . And who can honestly deny that race is a major reason America treats its poor more harshly than any other advanced country? . . . Consider this: in the United States, unlike any other advanced country, many people fail to receive basic health care because they can't afford it. Lack of health insurance kills many more Americans each year than Katrina and 9/11 combined. (A25)

The dramatic differences in the medical care of insured patients and uninsured patients were captured in the observation of Dr. Ruth Berggren, a physician at Charity Hospital in New Orleans when Hurricane Katrina struck. She recalled: "It was painful to watch helicopters ceaselessly evacuating insured patients from the roof of nearby Tulane Hospital while our 250 patients [at New Orleans' Charity Hospital] were evacuated by twos or threes in boats said to lead to buses that sometimes did not appear" (Associated Press 2005, A5).

Two of the authors of this volume taught children of poverty in a high-stakes test environment. We daily saw sick children who could not go home because there was no one there to care for them. Their mothers or guardians were working minimum-wage jobs in a poultry factory, a discount store, or at fast-food restaurants. They could not take off from work for fear of losing their jobs. There often were no cars available to pick up the children even if the parents or guardians could miss a half day or day of work. There was no nurse's room in our school building. Sick children had to put their heads down on their desks where we would try to make them as comfortable as possible. Teachers brought blankets for children who were ill and had chills. We tried to reduce fevers by putting moist paper towels on the children's foreheads. We saw ringworm, open sores, pus-filled sores, bleeding gums, rotting teeth, and heard rib-rattling coughs and whimpers of children in pain. A school nurse came only on Tuesday mornings. There were 611 children, grades pre-K through four in the school. Our pupils of poverty who suffered so much had to take the same high-stakes tests as children of affluence in Louisiana's wealthy neighborhoods and suburbs.

The home life of children of the excluded class can be miserable due to little or no heat in cold winter months; sweltering close quarters in hot, humid weather; and sharing space with rodents, roaches, and other pests. Lee (2006) reports, for example, that thousands of bedbugs plagued a Nyack, New York, mother and her five children. The bedbug infestation was one result of the family's lack of money. Lee explains:

> [The mother] could not afford to buy bedroom furniture for her sons. So she rented a bunk bed in July. That first week, mysterious bumps began appearing on her three sons' arms, legs and torsos. . . . Then medical complications arose. Her son Jair, 8, was allergic to the bites. His little bumps became infected and turned red and swollen. He was taken twice to the emergency room to lance angry boils on his torso. (B20)

Parent or guardian unemployment also can affect children in more ways than financial strain. Cottle (2001) observed that when breadwinners lose their jobs, family physical and mental problems can begin within fourteen days. He states:

> Insomnia, upset stomachs, ear and nasal infections, and all sorts of flu symptoms are reported almost at once and may strike any member of the family. Then there are the achy joints, back pains, and severe headaches felt by people, including children, who never have been sick a day in their lives. . . . Then there is the matter of psychological disturbances and outright mental illness that may be detected in any family member as a function of a father or mother being out of work for long periods of time. (19–20)

Unemployment is not exclusive to poor families, but the chances of finding a good paying job in a reasonable time frame are less for those with little education, transportation difficulties, and concern about daycare.

Rothstein (2004, 3) writes, "Lower-class children, on average, have poorer vision than middle-class children, partly because of prenatal conditions, partly because of how their eyes are trained as infants." We know from our classroom experience that if a child from the excluded class did get glasses to help him or her see, that child had better take care of them. Children in our classrooms told us that they had broken their glasses but could not get new ones because there was no money to do so. Some children cannot clearly see the high-stakes test items they must answer correctly. Rothstein also points out, "They [i.e., lower-class children] have poorer oral hygiene, more lead poisoning, more asthma, poorer nutrition, less adequate pediatric care, more exposure to smoke, and a host of other problems" (3).

When children with severe toothaches and no access to dental care must take the same high-stakes tests as children whose families receive "concierge care" from "boutique" physicians and dentists, something is wrong in this nation. When children must sleep in beds infested with bedbugs and endure the resultant infections and boils, they should not be subjected to high-stakes tests. When children of long-term unemployed parents must compete with children of well-employed parents, something is wrong with the accountability movement. When children with poor health, malnutrition, obesity caused by poverty, and no health insurance must take the same high-stakes tests as do children with robust health who eat the most nutritious foods in and out of school and who are fully insured, the deck is stacked. How can our state politicians and policymakers, the Business Roundtable, the U.S. Department of Education, our teacher education accreditors, our mayors and governors not see the injustice of holding all public school students to the same unproven standards as measured by the same skill-and-drill tests with such terrible consequences for the poor and the underserved? As a nation, we must demand an accounting from the elected and appointed officials who have set public education on this dangerous, unjust course. What are they thinking? Do they care so little about the poor, the excluded, and the ill that they deprive them of a real education so they can focus on raising test scores a point or two? When will these powerful people spend some real time—extended time—in the public schools so they can see the damage they have done?

Poverty and health are intertwined in every imaginable way. Poverty and violence also are intertwined as will be shown in the next chapter.

References

Alter, J. 2005. The other America. *Newsweek*, September 19, 42–48.

Ash, R. 2005. *The top 10 of everything 2006.* London, UK: Dorling Kindersley.

Associated Press. 2005. Doctors in disaster. *Newsday*, October 14, A5.

Bell, J., and M. Minaya. 2005. Race gap lingers in medical treatment. *Baltimore Sun*, August 18. www.baltimoresun.com (accessed August 18, 2005).

Belluck, P. 2005. Children's life expectancy being cut short by obesity. *New York Times,* March 17, A18.

Berthold, M. 2003. Dental Medicaid studied: Extensive review confirms children don't receive care. American Dental Assocation. www.ada.org/prof/resources/pubs/adanews/ (accessed December 3, 2005).

Block, R. W., and N. F. Krebs. 2005. Failure to thrive as a manifestation of child neglect. American Academy of Pediatrics. pediatrics.aappublications.org/cgi/content/full/116/5/1234 (accessed November 22, 2005).

Brewington, 2005. Bennett raises a storm. *Baltimore Sun,* October 1. www.baltimoresun.com (accessed October 1, 2005).

Calhoun School. 2005. Lunch menu. www.calhoun.org. (accessed January 1, 2006).

Child Trends Data Bank. 2005. Unmet dental needs. www.childtrendsdatabank.org/indicators/82UnmetDentalNeeds.cfm. (accessed December 3, 2005).

Children's Defense Fund. 2004. *Moments in America for children.* www.childrens defense.org/data/moments/aspx (accessed June 15, 2005).

———. 2005. The state of America's children 2005. www.childrensdefense.org/publications/greenbook/default.aspx (accessed November 24, 2005).

Chronicle of Higher Education. 2005. *Almanac of Higher Education 2005–2006.* August 26. Marion, OH: Chronicle of Higher Education.

Cottle, T. J. 2001. *Hardest times: The trauma of long-term unemployment.* Amherst: University of Massachusetts Press.

Dwight School. 2005. Lunch choices. www.dwight.edu/lunch_menu/main.html. (accessed January 4, 2006).

Epstein, H. 2003. Enough to make you sick? *New York Times Magazine,* October 12, 75, 79.

Fleck, C. 2006. Nothing to smile about. *AARP Bulletin,* September, 14–18.

Hanford, E. 2005. The trouble with teeth: Dental care and the problems of poverty. *North Carolina Public Radio,* April 18. www.wunc.org/voices/poverty/the-trouble-with-teeth-dental-care-and-the-problems-of-poverty (accessed December 3, 2005).

Harrington, M. 1962. *The other America: Poverty in the United States.* New York: Simon & Schuster, 1993.

Herbert, B. 2005. *Promises betrayed: Waking up from the American dream.* New York: Henry Holt and Company.

Homer (LA) Guardian-Journal. 2005. January 2–6 meal menu, December 22, 3B.

Johnson, D. D., and B. Johnson. 2006. *High stakes: Poverty, testing, and failure in American schools,* 2nd ed. Lanham, MD: Rowman & Littlefield.

Kids Count Data Book 2005: State Profiles of Child Well-Being. 2005. Baltimore, MD: Annie E. Casey Foundation.

Kristof, N. D. 2005. A health care disaster. *New York Times,* September 25, 11.

Krugman, P. 2005. Tragedy in black and white. *New York Times,* September 19, A25.

Lee, J. 2006. The bedbugs bite, and a family flees. *New York Times,* January 21, B20.

Morgan Quitno Press. 2005. Results of the 2005 healthiest state award. www .morganquitno.com/hc00fact.htm. (accessed October 14, 2005).

National Center for Education Statistics. 2005. The nation's report card: Reading. nces.ed.gov/nationsreportcard/reading. (accessed July 3, 2006).

Randall, V. R. 2005. Why race matters? University of Dayton. academic.udayton.edu/health/03access/data.htm (accessed October 14, 2005).

Rank, M. R. 2004. *One nation, underprivileged: Why American poverty affects us all.* Oxford, UK: Oxford University Press.

Rothstein, R. 2004. *Class and schools: Using social, economic, and educational reform to close the black-white achievement gap.* New York: Teachers College Columbia University and Washington, DC: Economic Policy Institute.

Samuels, C. A. 2006. Schools respond to federal "wellness" requirement. *Education Week*, June 14, 19, 21.

Sered, S. S., and R. Fernandopulle. 2005. *Uninsured in America.* Berkeley, CA: University of California Press.

Shields, M. 2005. Terrorists piling up victories in the war launched against them. *Naperville (IL) Daily Herald*, December 28, 18.

U.S. Department of Health and Human Services. National Institute of Dental and Craniofacial Research, National Institutes of Health. 2000. *Oral health in America: A report of the Surgeon General—Executive summary.* Rockville, MD: U.S. Department of Health and Human Services.

Viadero, D. 2006. Survey finds majority of elementary schools still offer recess time. *Education Week*, May 24, 14.

Wilkinson, R. 2005. *The impact of inequality: How to make sick societies healthier.* New York: New Press.

Zuger, A. 2005. For a retainer, lavish care by "boutique doctors." *New York Times*, October 30, 1, 26.

5

Violence and Safety Concerns in the Community, the School, and the Home

I N AN UNDERFUNDED SCHOOL THAT SERVES CHILDREN OF POVERTY, our third- and fourth-graders' lives were suffused with danger and violence. In the course of one school year, a pupil's brother was shot and killed, a mother was injured in a fistfight, another mother was put in jail for assault, a grandmother was brutally murdered by a knife-wielding crackhead, a pupil's cousin drowned, and three students lost everything in house fires. One child's father was in Angola, a maximum-security prison, for murder. Another child's father wore a tracking device on his ankle. Some pupils were kept awake until 2:30 A.M. because of noisy neighborhoods; others endured whippings and pressure to view violent "entertainment." One child saw his "real dad" choke and kick the boy's mother. Several of the children expressed fears about the Ku Klux Klan. We were told that many of the children came from environments where verbal abuse was the norm. "All they are used to is people shouting at them," an aide and local resident said (Johnson and Johnson 2006, 37).

The children witnessed alcohol and drug abuse. When a third-grader was asked if his mother could help him with his homework, the child replied, "No. When I get home, she drunk. . . . Every day she drunk or gone" (74). Later in the day, when asked about the child's home life, the assistant principal said that the mother was "a dopehead" and still was "a drunk." The administrator added, "You'll get no help from there" (74). During Drug Awareness Week, a fourth-grader wrote: "Drug affect my family by [my] dad do all kinds of drug. He do dope and wed [weed]. My uncle do wed. It just hurt my hart [heart]. I feel like one day they going to get the wrong thing. When my dad had smoke wed he try to burn my grandmother house. I was crying when my dad tried to burn up my grandmother house and he live there"(68). There was no school counselor; the teachers and children had to assume that role.

These conditions are not unusual in poor communities. Although children of all socioeconomic groups may witness or experience alcohol and drug abuse, those with money are better able to get professional help for their addictions. Few would argue that children of poverty see more real-life violence firsthand and live in more dangerous conditions than do more privileged children.

Two Types of Danger

For over half a century, psychologists have known that some needs take precedence over others. An individual must meet physiological needs (e.g., the need for food and water) first; the need for safety and security follows. If safety and security needs are not met, the individual cannot progress to cognitive needs such as the need to know and understand information. Garbarino, Dubrow, Kostelny, and Pardo (1992) define two "senses" of danger. The first type or "sense" is the probability that something bad will happen in a specific situation. The probability that a country club member will be a victim of violence during a well-guarded, invitation-only, private club event is small. The probability that a child who lives in a drug-infested neighborhood will see a violent act is much greater. The other type of danger is what Garbarino et al. call a subjective, "feeling of impending harm" (4). A tourist may feel uneasy on a South Bronx street late at night even though nothing "bad" may happen to that person. Southern black children's looming fear of the Ku Klux Klan would fit this type of danger. Garbarino et al. state, "Threats to a child's physical health can jeopardize mental and emotional development. Trauma can stunt intellectual development and impose stress that undermines social development" (10). Children of poverty who live among real or perceived violence and who fear for their physical safety are at developmental disadvantages that are certain to affect their classroom and test performances.

Dangers in the Community

Community violence, according to Linares (2006, 1), "refers to exposure, as a witness or through actual experience, to acts of interpersonal violence perpetrated by individuals who are not intimately related to the victim." Children who must live in violent communities endure stress that more affluent children do not experience. Poor children hear the sounds of violence: shouting, screaming, bullets being fired, sirens. They see the signs of violence: shock, injuries, weapons, death, weeping. Children who witness community violence may exhibit posttraumatic stress disorders not unlike those found in soldiers returning from battle (Linares 2006; Edelman 1992). Garbarino and his colleagues state that the more violence that children witness, the more mental disorders they exhibit. Symptoms can appear in the classroom even at the earliest ages. Garbarino et al. (1992, 56), in a discussion of research on community violence, found that children who live in violent areas show:

1. Difficulty in concentrating, because of lack of sleep and intrusive imagery
2. Memory impairment, because of avoidance or intrusive thoughts
3. Anxious attachment with their mothers, being fearful of leaving them or of sleeping alone
4. Aggressive play including imitating behaviors they have seen, as well as showing a desperate effort to protect themselves
5. Tough actions to hide their fears
6. Uncaring behavior resulting from experiencing hurt and loss
7. Severe constriction in activities, exploration, and thinking, for fear of re-experiencing the traumatic event

The authors of this volume who taught elementary school in a violent community saw the ramifications in the pupils. After a third-grader's family member was murdered, for example, the child seemed just to go though the motions of living. He mostly kept his head on his desk when he was not being addressed. The child, prior to the tragedy, was an energetic, creative boy who readily answered questions and had an easy smile. His sadness permeated the classroom because the other children knew why he was so distraught.

Interviewee Phyllis Forester, a teacher in a low-income Sacramento school, observed a young male beating a female, presumably his girlfriend, outside the school. The young girl took a baseball bat and smashed the boyfriend's car in front of the school. This scenario occurred while students were out for recess. Garbarino et al. write, "For poor children who already risk academic failure for cultural reasons, community violence is often scholastically the last straw" (59).

Consequences of community violence include gangs and for many, prison. Children and adolescents must satisfy the need for safety in some way, and too often that way is through gang membership. As irrational as it may seem, the gang provides security amidst chaos, self-esteem amidst hopelessness. Phillips (1999, 68) comments: "Because gang membership begins in childhood, heightened poverty rates among minors, combined with the lack of general opportunity they see around them, are crucial factors that perpetuate gang systems and the economic opportunities they provide. . . . Once they turn to gang membership, adoption of that system cuts them off even further from the meager opportunities that exist." Gang membership provides what the community and many homes cannot: protection, respect, support, pride, and even some spending money—however ill gotten.

But gangs engender violence. Sarah Young, a New York middle school reading teacher with 26 years of experience, talked about violence in her school's neighborhood. She said: "Violence is a common occurrence in this area. There are several gangs. There are often fights in school. There have been some instances of fighting with weapons, mostly knives. Since I have been here, there have been several murders in the area."

Carrie Brown, a Queens mother of teenage children, commented:

> There are lots of scary things that happen in the school: shootings, stabbings—there are fights all the time. Julian [her son] has a hard time because he breaks the rules by hanging out with the black kids. He is friends with a black gang but not in it. They fight pretty heavily with the Spanish gangs, which makes Julian a target; they feel that he is unfaithful to his race. There are Bloods and Crips and several other gangs in the school. One child a couple of weeks ago was cut with a machete.

How can students who witness beatings, stabbings, shootings, and machete attacks concentrate on their studies or preparation for high-stakes tests?

Phillips (1999, 69–70) states, "The United States is in the process of building the largest juvenile and adult prison system in the world. It currently jails more of its own people than most countries, rivaled only by such governments as China and Stalinist Russia. . . . Prisons are California's new aerospace—the single fastest growing industry in the state." Phillips argues that prison gangs and street gangs are inextricably woven together. It is not difficult to imagine that gang members find one another behind bars and strengthen their street gang allegiances during their incarceration.

The notion of having a prison in one's community apparently is not met with opposition in some needy areas. Prisons have sprung up in small, rural communities where family farms can no longer compete with corporate farms or in communities that have lost a major employer. When one travels Highway 29 in rural Wisconsin, for example, one is struck by an imposing, tan structure that seems incongruent with the otherwise bucolic scenery. The structure, the Stanley Correctional Institution, is the town's big business in an otherwise bleak economic vista. One cannot pass such a facility without wondering why we cannot or will not prevent adults from ending up in one of the 750 cells. We have years of research showing us the way, but no politician has been dogged enough to undertake the mission. Until someone in power takes the lead, prisons will continue to be the places where perpetrators of community violence end up and begin again. The warden of a Louisiana prison said, "I wish we would be put out of business. If some of the money shoveled into our end of the pipeline could be rerouted to children for food, decent housing, and well-equipped schools with current textbooks, maybe we could begin to be put out of business" (Johnson and Johnson 2006, 10).

There are environmental dangers associated with living in economically blighted communities where violence is commonplace. In rough urban areas, traffic and parking behaviors may pose threats to children walking to and from school. Abandoned buildings pose threats such as crumbling staircases and lurking drug users. There are no welcoming places to play outdoors for many children living in low-income communities, and even if there were, there would be worries about venturing out on crime-ridden streets. It is not just the criminals, however, that keep young children indoors on warm, sunny days.

Safety issues and health issues, discussed in the previous chapter, often overlap. Heavy traffic, common to urban areas, produces more vehicle exhaust. Industrial polluters emitting toxic wastes more often are found in poor communities; they would not be allowed in moneyed suburbs. In poor rural areas, livestock "containment" areas and garbage dumps dot the landscape and foul the air. If there is a failure in the waste "lagoons," the ground water is contaminated. Bullard (2005, 1) writes: "Historically, African American and other people of color communities have borne a disproportionate burden of pollution from incinerators, smelters, sewage treatment plants, chemical industries, and a host of other polluting facilities. . . . Environmental racism has rendered millions of blacks 'invisible' to government regulations and enforcement." Bullard discusses a study by the Associated Press (AP) that analyzed Environmental Protection Agency research. The AP found that African Americans "are 79 percent more likely than whites to live in neighborhoods where industrial pollution is suspected of posing the greatest health danger" (1). Bullard refers to these areas as environmental "sacrifice zones." Within these sacrifice zones, he reports that 600,000 students—mostly children of color—attend schools that are within a half a mile of "state-identified contaminated sites" (2).

Busy airports usually are not located in affluent neighborhoods because of noise concerns. Researchers have found that children who must endure aircraft noise have additional learning obstacles. Gary Evans, a Cornell professor, and his colleagues state that "noise exposure is consistently linked to reading deficits and may interfere with speech perception and long-term memory in primary school children" (Lang 2002, 1). Other researchers have found that "noise may also affect general health or sleep patterns, which can interfere with learning" (Bakalar 2005, F6).

A simple walk to school can pose more dangers. One of the authors of this volume was a volunteer at an all-black, low-income elementary school for a year. The principal of the school repeatedly asked the school board for a fence around a drainage ditch that was adjacent to the school. She feared that a young child might fall into the ditch and drown. It took many months and a lot of persistence before the board finally approved of a fence around the ditch. If the school had been in a prosperous neighborhood, it would not have been built near a drainage ditch, or if it had, the ditch would have been fenced immediately.

Safety at School

Pupils in contemporary schools face a number of safety issues including bullying by other students and threats of weapons use on or near school grounds. Information from the U.S. Department of Justice, compiled by the University of Virginia's Youth Violence Project (2006), revealed that minority pupils have more fear "at school or on the way to school" than white pupils. In some schools, free-for-alls can threaten student—and teacher—safety. One of our graduate students who teaches in a low-income, mostly minority urban New York school, recalled:

> Gangs are a very real problem in our district and added to the fighting that went on in the school. Whenever a fight took place in the school (and there were many), 80 percent of the student body would run through the halls to follow the fight. From outside the building, all you heard was the roar. During those altercations, when students barreled through the halls, teachers were supposed to stand against the walls. I, being a new teacher at the time, didn't realize the protocol, and found myself being carried and trampled upon (up a stairway) during one of those events. Fortunately, another teacher nearby was able to grab my hand to pull me out and against the wall.

Some students in low-income neighborhoods must leave school premises and contend with urban traffic on mean streets just to use a restroom. Gootman (2004, B3) reports, "At Abraham Lincoln High School in Brooklyn, the bathrooms are so bad that students have been known to use the toilets at Coney Island hospital, down the road."

Poor children are more likely to attend old, vermin-infested schools where needed repairs are put on hold and teachers and staff use patch jobs to keep their students safe. Rodents and cockroaches are not uncommon in these buildings. Johnson and Johnson (2006) write that they frequently stepped on roaches in their classrooms in broad daylight—an indication that the roach population in the school was large. Cockroaches, according to the Minnesota Department of Agriculture (2006), "are known to carry human pathogens and can potentially transmit diseases to people. Additionally, cockroaches are a source of allergens and can cause allergic reactions and asthma in people, especially children."

In some poor school districts, the buildings themselves actually could collapse on the pupils. Melmer (2004, 1–3) found this perilous situation on the Crow Creek Reservation in South Dakota:

> Imagine rodents and snakes dropping in for classroom activities with elementary students, rain drops on desks unimpaired by a roof, no running water in a science lab and attending school in a fire trap. . . . The Crow Creek High School building, located just north of Fort Thompson, the largest town on the reservation, has a frame structure attached to the outside walls with building long rods. When the rods are tightened they keep the outside walls from collapsing. . . . The elementary school . . . is completely unsafe and the state fire marshal gave the school 90 days to upgrade the school to meet fire code. . . . Should a fire start in the kitchen, the fire alarms and the sprinkler system would not work. . . . There are many days during the school year when school is either let out early or called off because of sewer backup, broken water pipes or other problems that become catastrophes. . . . Buffalo County, which encompasses the Crow Creek Reservation is the poorest county in the United States, measured by per capita income and growth in that number.

In Cleveland, a closed school in a dangerous neighborhood was reopened for elementary pupils because their elementary school's roof was "close to collapsing" (Okoben 2006, 1). Parents were worried about their children attending the reopened school because of gun violence in the neighborhood. Despite the children's situation and the disruptions caused by relocating to such a school, Okoben notes, "Losing at least eight days of instruction is a concern, especially with state proficiency tests looming in March."

Corporal Punishment

When children are in a secured classroom, they presumably are safe from physical harm. This is not the case in all classrooms—especially for poor and minority children. Although corporal punishment is illegal in 28 states, over 342,000 American students were hit in a school year by educators, according to the most recent data released by the U.S. Department of Education, Office for Civil Rights and compiled by the National Coalition to Abolish Corporal Punishment in Schools (NCACPS) (2006). It is not the distinguished white doctor's child or the successful white lawyer's child or the prominent white

CEO's child who is being hit in the public schools. It usually is the poor, minority child. Wilgoren (2001) found that "black students are 2.5 times as likely to be struck [by school personnel] as white students, a reflection of what researchers have long found to be more frequent and harsher discipline for members of minorities." Dobbs (2004) reports that Mississippi is the "top paddling state" where approximately 10 percent of its pupils are hit with a wooden paddle as a means of discipline: "In poorer parts of the state, where a higher proportion of children are from minority and single-parent families, the use of corporal punishment is even more frequent. . . . Studies have shown that there is a high correlation between paddling and poverty." A Mississippi assistant principal, who worked in a school where more than 90 percent of the children were eligible for free and reduced lunch, was told by the principal, "These kids are different, all they understand is the paddle . . . walk the halls and, if the kids are out of line, burn their butts." Those in favor of paddling a child often refer to the "spare the rod, spoil the child" school of thought. It appears, however, that the rod is spared if children are affluent and white. Johnson and Johnson (2006) reported that in the school where they taught, 80 percent of the pupils were African American. Paddling in the school was not uncommon. A shouting, scowling, white first grade teacher carried her paddle everywhere: escorting the tiny, fearful black children to the restrooms, to the playground, and to the gymnasium. A white male uncertified teacher paddled a little girl until she wet her pants.

Mississippi, Arkansas, Alabama, Tennessee, Oklahoma, Louisiana, Texas, Georgia, Missouri, and New Mexico are "the 10 worst states" in the percentage of students hit each year (NCACPS 2006). Most industrialized nations have outlawed corporal punishment, and many professional organizations have spoken out against its use. These include the American Academy of Pediatrics, the American Medical Association, the American Psychiatric Association, the Council for Exceptional Children, the National Association of Elementary School Principals, the National Association of School Nurses, the National Association of State Boards of Education, the Association for Childhood Education International, and several others (NCACPS 2006). One voice is disturbingly silent—the National Council for Accreditation of Teacher Education (NCATE).

NCATE claims that up to 700 schools of education are NCATE accredited or are in the process of being accredited (NCATE n.d.). It currently has "partnerships" with 48 states, Puerto Rico, and Washington, DC. A few states mandate that all teacher education programs be NCATE accredited. The 22 states that permit corporal punishment are partner states with NCATE. We could find no statements from NCATE that discourage the striking of children in these states. This silence is even more unsettling in light of an NCATE boast,

"You know that NCATE does not exist simply to provide recognition to institutions; it exists for the public good—to help protect schoolchildren" (NCATE 2001, 2). If NCATE truly believes it is important to protect schoolchildren, it would insist that its partner states desist from the archaic and hurtful practice of beating children. Nadine Block of the Center for Effective Discipline points out, "Under U.S. law, children are the only class of individuals who can be legally hit" (Dobbs 2004).

A *professional development school* (PDS) is a school where student teachers are sent and university and public school faculty are encouraged to collaborate. Arthur Wise, the president of NCATE, and Marsha Levine, a director of NCATE's Professional Development Schools Standards Project state, "The PDS is to teacher preparation as the teaching hospital is to physician preparation, i.e., a new institution to provide high quality service to students while preparing new generations of teachers" (Wise and Levine 2002, 56). Are NCATE's PDSs preparing new generations of teachers to accept or use corporal punishment as a means of discipline? The American Medical Association's (AMA) (2006) position on corporal punishment in schools is clear: "The AMA (1) supports the abolition of corporal punishment in schools; [and] (2) encourages universities that train teachers to emphasize alternative forms of discipline during their training."

Unlike the AMA, we can find no evidence that NCATE has spoken out against corporal punishment, or has sanctioned its partner states who condone the practice, or has failed to accredit teacher preparation programs where hitting children is used as a form of discipline in schools that are sites for university practica or student teaching. In an essay that delineates the responsibilities of public intellectuals to speak out on critical issues, Henry A. Giroux (2006, 64) writes:

> Unfortunately, too many academics retreat into narrow specialisms, allow themselves to become adjuncts of the corporation, or align themselves with dominant interests that serve largely to consolidate authority rather than to critique its abuses. Refusing to take positions on controversial issues or to examine the role they might play in lessening human suffering, such academics become models of moral indifference and examples of what it means to disconnect learning from public life.

The refusal of NCATE and its academic "partners" to take a stand against corporal punishment is an example of moral indifference through alignment with dominant interests. This is not surprising in light of NCATE's 2006 decision to remove *social justice* from its vocabulary when NCATE came up for federal review for continued approval as an accreditor during the second term of George W. Bush's presidency (National Advisory Committee on Institutional Quality and Integrity 2006, 255).

The National Center for Education Statistics (2005) states: "In addition to experiencing loneliness, depression, and adjustment difficulties, victimized children are more prone to truancy, poor academic performance, and dropping out of school." Corporal punishment meted out by trusted school personnel should be viewed as victimization of young children who learn at school that hitting is used to solve problems. America's public schoolchildren are learning this lesson—whether as recipients or witnesses—every 13 seconds because that is how often a child is hit by a teacher or staff member (Children's Defense Fund 2004b).

Psychological Damage

In addition to the physical dangers poor minority children may encounter in the classroom, there are possible psychological dangers. These are associated with high-stakes testing. Some children are under such pressure to pass these tests that they now practice trying to rid their psyches of a monster—the "test monster." Herszenhorn (2006, B1) reports: "Stressed. Scared. Nauseous. Sick. These were some of the words that the nine- and ten-year-olds at Public School 3 in Brooklyn used on Friday to describe how they felt about the state fourth-grade reading test that they will take over three days beginning today. But that was before social workers introduced them to a Test Monster, an art project designed to exorcise fears of standardized tests." Herzenhorn writes that a nine-year-old child looked at his Test Monster and said, "Ooooh, I am going to hurt you!" (B1). A worker in the school noted, "Oftentimes you have kids who just fall apart during the test; they just start crying or having a temper tantrum" (B1). Is dealing with a Test Monster the way we want elementary pupils to spend their time? What is the testing doing to young children's mental health? What are the long-term effects of this type of pressure on such young children? Garbarino et al. (1992, 121) observe that if schools provide disadvantaged children with "a carefully designed, developmentally appropriate, and facilitative school experience . . . the potential for developmental delay or arrest from biological or psychological trauma" is reduced. The schools no longer provide this cushion for children from the excluded class.

Dangers at Home

For many children of the excluded class, home offers no solace. Housing units often are crowded and can be firetraps. Kilgannon (2005) reports that lack of money forced a single Queens mother to rent a portion of a basement for her five children and herself. At least 21 people lived in the house. When fire broke out one evening, three of the young children died in the blaze. A neighbor of the family remarked, "That basement is like most of the basements in this neighborhood: a death trap. . . . You have a thousand of them around here. Knock on any door." Relatives of the mother said that the home "had broken windows and electrical wires hanging from the ceiling" (B3).

Child Abuse

The most sickening betrayals of what homes are supposed to be are cases of child abuse and neglect, and poor children often are the victims of these betrayals. In an issue of *American Family Physician,* published by the American Academy of Family Physicians, Bethea (1999, 4) writes, "Poverty is the most frequently and persistently noted risk factor for child abuse. Physical abuse and neglect are more common among the people who are the poorest." Six years after Bethea's report, the Children's Defense Fund (2005, 115, 116) states: "Poverty is the best single predictor of child abuse and neglect. . . . Neglect is the form of child maltreatment where the link to poverty is most obvious, since it often can be directly tied to a family's lack of resources. . . . Poverty also may contribute to child abuse and neglect by adding stress to a family's life. The daily struggle to put food on the table and keep a roof overhead may be the proverbial straw that breaks the camel's back."

It is not difficult to find cases of child abuse and neglect in the daily newspapers of sleek cities or one-stoplight towns. Jefcoats (2006), in *The Atlanta Journal-Constitution,* reports that a father and stepmother were arrested for making their son hold a shovel over his head while the boy kneeled on concrete blocks. His injuries from this practice were noticed by relatives because the wounds had become infected. The father also hit the child in the stomach if he moved while holding the shovel. In Seattle, Clarridge (2004) writes that a father beat his nine-year-old son and eight-year-old daughter with "cable wire, sticks, belts and a wooden pole; pulled on their fingers and toenails with pliers;" and "put weights on their backs" (1). A Pineville, Louisiana, man was charged with killing his girlfriend's two-year-old boy (*Alexandria Town Talk* 2006). In New York City, a seven-year-old girl was killed by her stepfather for taking some yogurt out of the refrigerator and eating it. Barron and Baker (2006) write that the child, who was beaten to death, had endured "months of being systematically tortured and denied food" (B1). The child weighed less than 36 pounds when she died.

When a Bronx four-year-old tipped over a television set, he was beaten by his mother's boyfriend. Baker and Kaufman (2006) reported that after the boy was beaten, the family went to a chain restaurant where the child vomited blood. When the family returned, the boy was beaten again. Baker and Kaufman write that according to police reports, the man, "grabbed the boy's neck, pushed his face into the wall and grabbed him by the ankles, swung him and hurled him into the wall." The man also "had beaten the boy with his fists, a belt and a plastic bat." The child "suffered a fractured skull and a lacerated spleen and pancreas," and when he was found, the child "was lying on a mattress in a makeshift bedroom in the apartment's living room, bleeding from the ears and rectum" (B6). The child's two sisters were victims of neglect—not enough to eat and insufficient clothing. Baker and Kaufman remark that the family lived in "a squalid apartment where the police said cold air streamed in through a broken window, most of the children slept in a single room and there was little food in the refrigerator" (B1). The Children's Defense Fund (2004a) found that "2,482 children are confirmed as abused or neglected" every day in America. These are the numbers that are confirmed. There certainly must be incidents of unreported abuse and neglect. The deck is stacked against abused, neglected victims of violence who must take the same high-stakes tests as children of affluence who come to school fresh from summer camp, fine trips, or other costly diversions.

The U.S. Department of Health and Human Services (2006) reports that "maltreatment during infancy or early childhood can cause important regions of the brain to form improperly, leading to physical, mental, and emotional problems such as sleep disturbances, panic disorder, and attention-deficit/hyperactivity disorder." Bethea (1999), in an American Academy of Family Physicians publication, explains several consequences of child abuse. She points out "delays in reaching developmental milestones" and writes, "children who receive maltreatment in these early years may actually have suboptimal brain development." These problems are ignored by policymakers and politicians who support conformity in classroom accomplishments. The U.S. Department of Health and Human Services (2006) notes that "protective factors" such as "adequate housing," "access to health care," and "parental employment" can lessen the risks of maltreatment; however, these factors often are missing in poor people's lives.

Even if a child is not a direct victim of abuse, what are the effects of witnessing domestic violence? The National Clearinghouse on Child Abuse and Neglect Information (U.S. Department of Health and Human Services 2003) states:

Childhood problems associated with exposure to domestic violence fall into three primary categories:

- Behavioral, social, and emotional problems: Higher levels of aggression, anger, hostility, oppositional behavior, and disobedience; fear, anxiety, withdrawal, and depression; poor peer, sibling, and social relationships; and low self-esteem

- Cognitive and attitudinal problems: Lower cognitive functioning, poor school performance, lack of conflict resolution skills, limited problem solving skills, pro-violence attitudes, and belief in rigid gender stereotypes and male privilege
- Long-term problems: Higher levels of adult depression and trauma symptoms and increased tolerance for and use of violence in adult relationships

Politicians, who seem to be keen on "scientifically-based research" to improve what they believe are ailing schools, should have no trouble locating the vast number of studies that show the damage done to children who live in unsafe and violent surroundings.

There are steps politicians can take to ease these societal maladies, but none of these steps involves high-stakes testing and the mental beatings poor children must take when they suspect that they cannot pass these tests because of all the factors discussed in this book. Bethea (1999) suggested years ago that families should be helped in becoming economically self-sufficient and that health care become less expensive and more available. These things have not happened. There are well-paid experts who examine and debate test results, vendors who promise higher test scores, and politicians who brag about a few measly test points that are educationally insignificant. There are persistent voices, unheeded so far, who say that until poverty is addressed, children of the excluded class will come up short in school. Zigler writes: "The problems of many families will not be solved by early intervention efforts, but only by changes in the basic features of the infrastructure of our society. No amount of counseling, early childhood curricula, or home visits will take the place of jobs that provide decent incomes, affordable housing, appropriate health care, optimal family configurations, or integrated neighborhoods where children can encounter positive role models" (Garbarino et al. 1992, 118). Until corrective justice is established, we can count on seeing more tiny victims of frightening neighborhoods, nightmarish home environments, and schools where problems are tackled with a wooden paddle.

References

Alexandria (LA) Town Talk. 2006. Our view: Child abuse statistics a cry for help. January 14. www.thetowntalk.com/ (accessed January 15, 2006).

American Medical Association. (AMA). 2006. H-515.995: Corporal punishment in schools. www.ama-assn.org (accessed January 25, 2006).

Bakalar, N. 2005. Jumbo jets can drown out Dick and Jane. *New York Times,* June 14, F6.

Baker, A., and L. Kaufman. 2006. City was told six times of trouble in Bronx boy's home. *New York Times,* February 1, B1, B6.

Barron, J., and A. Baker. 2006. Bloomberg orders inquiry in death of abused girl, 7. *New York Times*, January 14, B1, B4.

Bethea, L. 1999. Primary prevention of child abuse. *American Family Physician*, March 15. www.aafp.org/afp/990315ap/1577.html (accessed January 18, 2006).

Bullard, R. D. 2005. More blacks overburdened with dangerous pollution: AP study of EPA risk scores confirms two decades of EJ findings. Environmental Justice Resource Center. www.ejrc.cau.edu/BullardAPEJ.html (accessed January 20, 2006).

Children's Defense Fund. 2004a. Each day in America. www.childrensdefense.org/data/eachday.aspx (accessed June 15, 2005).

———. 2004b. Moments in America for children. www.childrensdefensefund.org/data/moments.aspx (accessed June 15, 2005).

———. 2005. State of America's children 2005. www.childrensdefense.org/publications/greenbook/default.aspx.

Clarridge, C. 2004. Father pleads guilty to child abuse, faces 18-year term. *Seattle Times*, December 2. seattletimes.nwsource.com/html/localnews/ (accessed February 2, 2006).

Dobbs, M. 2004. U.S. students still getting the paddle—Corporal punishment laws often reflect regional chasms. *Washington Post*, February 24. www.nospank.net/n-151r.htm (accessed January 23, 2006).

Edelman, M. W. 1992. *The measure of our success*. New York: HarperPerennial.

Garbarino, J., N. Dubrow, K. Kostelny, and C. Pardo. 1992. *Children in danger: Coping with the consequences of community violence*. San Francisco: Jossey-Bass.

Giroux, H. A. 2006. Higher education under siege: Implications for public intellectuals. *Thought and Action* 22 (Fall): 63–78.

Gootman, E. 2004. Dirty and broken bathrooms make for a long school day. *New York Times*, January 29, B3.

Herszenhorn, D. M. 2006. Toughening up for tests: As stakes rise, schools try to ease the anxiety. *New York Times*, January 10, B1, B5.

Jefcoats, K. 2006. McDonough couple charged with child cruelty. *Atlanta Journal-Constitution*, January 14, 2006. www.ajc.com/ (accessed January 15, 2006).

Johnson, D. D., and B. Johnson. 2006. *High stakes: Poverty, testing, and failure in American schools*. 2d ed. Lanham, MD: Rowman & Littlefield.

Kilgannon, C. 2005. Four dead in Queens: A story of poverty, crowding and fire. *New York Times*, December 8, B3.

Lang, S. 2002. CU study finds airport noise impairs children's memory and reading ability. *Cornell Chronicle*. October 17. www.newscornell.edu/Chronicle/ (accessed January 30, 2006).

Linares, L. O. 2006. Community violence: The effects on children. New York University Child Study Center. www.aboutourkids.org/aboutour/articles/communityviolence.html (accessed January 20, 2006).

Melmer, D. 2004. Crow Creek: Unsafe schools. *Indian Country Today*. www.indiancountry.com (accessed January 24, 2006).

Minnesota Department of Agriculture. 2006. Cockroaches. www.mda.state.mn.us/IPM/fsschcockroach.pdf (accessed January 24, 2006).

National Advisory Committee on Institutional Quality and Integrity. 2006. Transcript on hearing for continued approval: National Council for Accreditation of Teacher Education. U.S. Department of Education: Washington, DC.

National Center for Education Statistics. 2005. Indicators of school crime and safety: 2005. nces.ed.gov/programs/crimeindicators/ (accessed January 24, 2006).

National Coalition to Abolish Corporal Punishment in Schools (NCACPS). 2006. Discipline at school. www.stophitting.com/disatschool/facts.php (accessed January 22, 2006).

National Council for Accreditation of Teacher Education (NCATE). 2001. A decade of growth 1991–2001. www.ncate.org/newsbrfs/dec_report.htm (accessed January 11, 2004).

———. n.d. Making a difference. www.ncate.org/documents/NCATENews/NCATE Impacts.pdf (accessed January 30, 2006).

Okoben, J. 2006. Roof collapse danger closes Cleveland school. *Cleveland Plain Dealer*, January 6, 2006. www.cleveland.com (accessed January 24, 2006).

Phillips, S. A. 1999. *Wallbangin': Graffiti and gangs in L.A.* Chicago: University Chicago Press.

U.S. Department of Health and Human Services. National Clearinghouse on Child Abuse and Neglect Information. 2003. Children and domestic violence: A bulletin for professionals. nccanch.acf.hhs.gov/pubs/factsheets/domestic violence.cfm (accessed February 2, 2006).

———. Centers for Disease Control and Prevention, National Center for Injury Prevention and Control. 2006. Child maltreatment: Fact sheet. www.cdc.gov/ncipc/factsheets/cmfacts.htm (accessed January 19, 2006).

University of Virginia. Virginia Youth Violence Project. n.d. youthviolence.edschool .virginia.edu/violence-in-schools/national-statistics.html (accessed January 25, 2006).

Wilgoren, J. 2001. Lawsuits touch off debate over paddling in schools. *New York Times,* May 3. www.corpun.com/uss00105.htm.

Wise, A. E., and M. Levine. 2002. The 10-step solution: Helping urban districts boost achievement in low-performing schools. *Education Week,* February 27, 38, 56.

6

School Funding Inequities

When Matt Schrimpf graduates from Centennial High in Williamson County this month, he'll do so as valedictorian, with 27 hours of college credit under his belt, experience in jazz band and the school's debate team and the prospect of a promising education at Harvard University. When Beth Marin graduates as valedictorian of Hancock County High in Sneedville, she'll do so with no experience in trigonometry class, physics, music or art classes. She will have had no Advanced Placement courses. . . . "I'm afraid I'm behind," said Beth, who has a perfect 4.0 grade-point average. Both students will graduate at the top of their class from Tennessee public schools funded by Tennessee taxpayers, but their educations are further apart than the 271 miles that separate their schools. (Klausnitzer 2004)

The "Best" High Schools

EACH YEAR *NEWSWEEK* MAGAZINE PUBLISHES A LIST of "America's Best High Schools." One thousand high schools are ranked on the *Newsweek* website (xtra.Newsweek.com), and the top 100 are named and ranked in the paper publication. *Newsweek* uses a formula to recognize "schools that do the best job of preparing average students for college" (Kantrowitz and Wingert 2006, 54). It does this by dividing the number of Advanced Placement (AP) and International Baccalaureate (IB) tests taken at a school by the number of graduating seniors. *Newsweek* believes that this number is an indicator of "how committed a school is to helping kids take college-level courses" (4). This procedure rules out schools that do not, for a variety of reasons, make AP or IB classes available. Valedictorian Beth Marin of Hancock County High in Sneedville, Tennessee, was a student in such a school.

It is not surprising that most of the "best" schools serve primarily children of the affluent. In 41 of the schools, fewer than 11 percent are on free or reduced lunch. In 62 of the schools, 20 percent or fewer of the students qualify for free or reduced lunch. In only six of the "best" schools do more than half the students qualify. The determination of who qualifies for free or reduced lunch is based on federal poverty levels of family income (see chapter 3).

This chapter examines the historical precedence of public law and the government programs that created today's fiscal inequities in public education. Our current education system is the result of court decisions, complex school finance formulae, and politics. The intentional or unintentional effects of social and economic decisions, programs, and attitudes have given rise to a caste system of education in the United States.

Court Decisions

In 1850 the Supreme Court of Massachusetts, in the case of *Roberts v. City of Boston*, upheld the Boston School Committee's decision to maintain segregated schools. *Plessy v. Ferguson* (1896) challenged the "separate but equal" doctrine under the Equal Protection Clause of the Fourteenth Amendment (Alexander and Alexander 1984; La Morte 1990; Neville 1986). This case reviewed previous arguments in the earlier Massachusetts case prior to the passage of the Fourteenth Amendment of the U.S. Constitution in 1868. Similar to the Massachusetts decision, *Plessy v. Ferguson* was upheld at the federal level. Plessy provided the legal basis for a dual school system separated by race. The school systems in which black and white students were segregated was only one of the law's outcomes. This decision also led to the enactment of Jim Crow laws in many areas of public life (see chapter 2). The pernicious nature of the decision was not lost on all the Supreme Court justices. Justice John Marshall Harlan's dissenting opinion states, in part:

> There is no caste here. Our Constitution is color-blind, and neither knows nor tolerates classes among citizens. In respect of civil rights, all citizens are equal before the law. The humblest is the peer of the most powerful. The law regards man as man, and takes no account of his surroundings or of his color when his civil rights as guaranteed by the supreme law of the land are involved. It is, therefore, to be regretted that this high tribunal, the final expositor of the fundamental law of the land, has reached the conclusion that it is competent for a State to regulate the enjoyment by citizens of their civil rights solely upon the basis of race. (usinfo.state.gov n.d.)

Justice Harlan's concerns were not revisited until 1954 when the United States Supreme Court decision in *Brown v. Board of Education* reversed the *Plessy* decision. In this case, it was recognized that the "separate but equal" doctrine was inherently unconstitutional. It was apparent to most who studied the assets of predominantly minority schools that there was no equity with those of the wealthier predominantly white schools.

In spite of the *Brown* decision, the move to desegregate schools has been slow and has led to two tests to determine the legality of segregation: de jure and de facto. De jure segregation is segregation created by law. De facto segregation is segregation according to factual data. For example, all-black neighborhoods can be viewed as de facto segregation. The prevalence of all-black public schools in some towns where there is a white population can be considered de facto segregation. In de facto segregated school districts, white parents often send their children to "academies" where tuition costs rule out children of the excluded class (Johnson and Johnson 2006).

In 1973 the U.S. Supreme Court (*San Antonio Independent School District v. Rodriguez*) ruled that the allocation of school funds based on property taxes was not a violation of the Equal Protection Clause of the Fourteenth Amendment (caselaw.findlaw.com n.d.) For all intents and purposes, the decision shut the door on federal sponsorship of equality of education funding.

It has been suggested that the de facto/de jure distinction should be eliminated and replaced with a national policy to address segregation (La Morte 1990). It should make no difference whether the cause or effect of segregation was created, assisted, or perpetuated by the state. Statistical evidence reveals that large minority populations are clustered in economically depressed regions, whether these are urban, suburban, or rural areas. Case decisions such as *Green v. County School Board of New Kent County, Virginia* (1968) and *Swann v. Charlotte-Mecklenburg Board of Education* (1971) in North Carolina took steps in moving toward a unitary system of education (Ancheta 2004). The districts had "the affirmative duty to take whatever steps might be necessary to convert to a unitary system in which racial discrimination would be eliminated root and branch" (La Morte 1990, 332). Without being able to prove segregation acts and intent to segregate, however, the outcome of cases such as *Milliken v. Bradley* (1974) in the state of Michigan still leave large urban centers such as Detroit 81.6 percent black. At the same time, the surrounding suburbs remain majority white (Hazel Park, 90.4 percent; Ferndale, 90.4 percent; Huntington Woods, 96.3 percent; Pleasant Ridge, 95.3 percent; Centerline, 92.8 percent) (U.S. Census Bureau 2002).

Even though the courts have distinguished between de facto and de jure segregation, both forms perpetuate segregated communities. Local zoning laws, which prevent affordable housing in many wealthy suburbs or housing policies that concentrate subsidized housing in urban centers, divide communities based on race and economics. The lesson learned from case law is that the Constitution forbids any governmental structure from practicing segregation, but it does not require integration to remedy a situation caused by "unfortunate economics."

According to the U.S. Constitution, education is the right of the state, and the federal government intercedes only when an individual's civil liberties have been violated. This wiggle room has exacerbated differences in economic and educational opportunities for many minorities. In a political era when constitutional amendments have been proposed to ban flag burning and gay marriage, no amendment has been proposed to equalize funding for America's schoolchildren.

School Funding

A *Newsday* headline said it all: "Hempstead reduced its budget by 12.5% and Roslyn added three tennis courts." The 2005–2006 school budget of Roslyn, New York, included the following expenditures:

- $400,000 for three tennis courts
- $45,000 for three water fountains ($15,000 each)
- $80,000 for a lawn sprinkler system
- Gold leaf for the back of the aisle seats in the auditorium
- $300,000 for Astroturf for the high school
- Line items for consultants
- More air-conditioned buses with tinted windows. (roslyntaxpayer.com 2006, 1)

Hempstead and Roslyn are only miles apart on Long Island, but the differences in family incomes and therefore school budgets are enormous. In a reference to scandals in both school districts, Applebome (2005) compares Roslyn to "a gilded-age tale of excess ripe for at least Tom Wolfe" and Hempstead to a tale by Elmore Leonard with ills that are "dispiriting, endless—not a single event but a doleful, seemingly intractable status quo" (25). Children in both districts take the same New York and federal-government mandated high-stakes tests.

Based on information from the U.S. Census Bureau, we examine K–12 education revenues in four ways. Comparisons are made on a state-by-state basis; on tax revenues provided by local, state, and federal governments; on the expenditures by public elementary and secondary schools; and on the distribution of the current spending on instruction and support services. The annual survey of local government finances of the U.S. Census Bureau (2005) demonstrates the wide range of states' spending per pupil for elementary-secondary

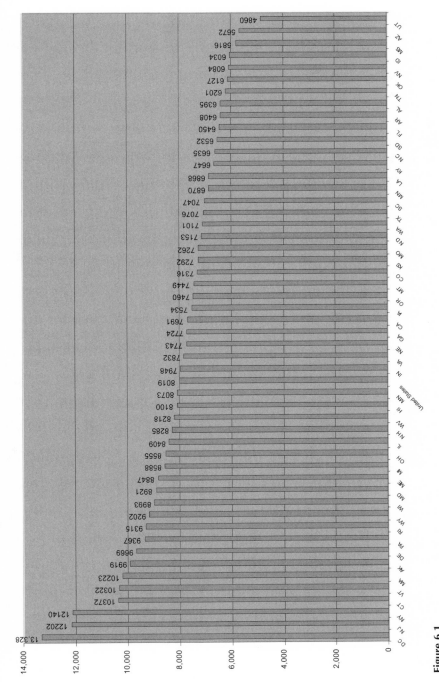

Figure 6.1
Current Spending per Pupil for Elementary-Secondary Education by State: 2002–2003 (U.S. Census Bureau 2005)

education (figure 6.1). Interstate comparisons exemplify this variability. The District of Columbia, New Jersey, and New York spend above $10,000 per pupil, but Mississippi, Arizona, and Utah spend less than $6,000 per pupil. The difference between the highest per pupil spending in the District of Columbia and the lowest per pupil spending in Utah is $8,468 per student per year.

The total reported revenue for public K–12 education was $440.3 billion for 2002–2003 (figure 6.2). Nationally, federal sources provide 8 percent of the total cost for K–12 education, while state sources provide 49 percent and local sources provide 43 percent (U.S. Census Bureau 2005). Ninety percent of local revenue is from property taxes. These statistics reveal the importance of and the reliance on local revenues to fund education. This reliance contributes to the chasm that exists between the wealth of school districts.

The 2002–2003 school year expenditures on public education for K–12 students were $453.6 billion (U.S. Census Bureau 2005). There are three categories of expenditures: *current spending*, which is approximately $389.9 billion (or 86 percent of the budget); *capital outlay*, which is approximately $50.4 billion (or 11.1 percent of the budget); and *other expenditures* accounting for approximately $13.2 billion (or 2.9 percent of the budget) (figure 6.3). The largest category, current spending, is subdivided and includes instruction (approximately 61 percent), support services (approximately 34 percent), and other (approximately 5 percent). The next largest expenditure is capital outlay. Capital outlay refers to expenses involving construction of buildings and roads, purchasing of equipment and land, and payments on leases.

A total of $389.9 billion was spent on instruction and support services for K–12 education in the 2002–2003 school year. The money allocated to instruction pays for salaries, benefits, contributions to retirement funds, purchased services, supplies, and daily maintenance. Support services are subdivided into pupil support, administration, maintenance, and transportation (Carr 2005; Klurfield 2006).

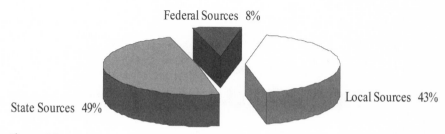

Figure 6.2
Percent Distribution of Public Elementary-Secondary Education Revenue: 2002–2003, Total: $440.3 billion

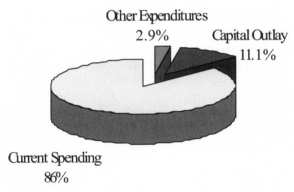

Figure 6.3
Percent Distribution of Public Elementary-Secondary Education
Expenditure: 2002–2003, Total: $453.6 billion

The method of financing education is proving to be more and more unsatisfactory to local residents as the costs of education rise and the return of tax dollars from the state decreases. The Campaign for Fiscal Equity, based in New York City, reported that only five of 50 states—Delaware, Hawaii, Mississippi, Nevada, and Utah—have not had litigation challenging the constitutionality of funding practices for elementary and secondary education (Kennedy 2005).

What is the local difference? Districts with few commercial or industrial properties shift the entire local tax burden of funding education to homeowners in that community (Hawaii is an exception). The tax levy is expressed as a percentage based on the value of the property. Consequently, expensive properties can generally raise more money at a lower tax burden to the homeowner. The wealth of a particular school district usually is measured by a funding formula that includes the total amount of taxable property divided by the number of students served in that district (La Morte 1990; Neville 1986). For example, District A has a taxable assessed valuation of $800,000 per student. Assuming that the tax levy is $10 per $1,000 of property value, District A would raise $8,000 for every $800,000 of assessed property. District B, however, has a taxable assessed valuation of $90,000 per student. Assume the tax levy is still $10 per $1,000 of property value. In contrast to District A, District B would raise $900 for every $90,000 of assessed property. In this example, the finance formula has a negative impact on District B.

What is the magic number for the finance formula? School district funding is costly, complicated, and unpredictable. Figuring out education finance formulae at the state level is like playing with a Rubik's Cube. States have numerous tax exceptions when calculating local education budgets. General allowances include incentives for heavily taxed communities, poor districts with low tax bases, and more. Further, school funding is highly political and the amount of the funds available depends on each individual state's annual budget. At the community level, when state budgets are not adopted in a timely manner (the fiscal year usually ending on June 30), school districts do not receive their needed operating funds. This requires districts to borrow money and incur additional debt to finance their obligations. For individuals with the financial capital, purchasing the school-based short-term notes is a good investment. For the district, however, this practice only increases the cost of education (Educational Priorities Panel 2000; McGuire 1990; Scheuer 1999).

There is no limit on the amount of money a community can spend on education. In fact, cases brought before courts that have argued solely for equal spending among districts have not fared well. A change in the tactic where plaintiffs challenge the adequacy of funding has proven to be more successful. Kennedy (2005, 1) reports, "Since 1989, plaintiffs have won 23 of 27 cases that were based on adequacy arguments." Adequacy arguments require that plaintiffs determine the price of what is considered a sound and basic education. New York State Supreme Court Justice Leland DeGrasse defines what a sound, basic education entails:

- sufficient numbers of qualified teachers, principals, and other personnel
- appropriate class sizes
- adequate and accessible school buildings with sufficient space to ensure appropriate class size and implementation of a sound curriculum
- sufficient and up-to-date books, supplies, libraries, educational technology and laboratories
- suitable curricula, including an expanded platform of programs to help at-risk students by giving them "more time on task"
- adequate resources for students with extraordinary needs
- a safe orderly environment (Educational Priorities Panel 2001)

Twenty-three states (Alaska, Arizona, Connecticut, Georgia, Idaho, Kansas, Kentucky, Louisiana, Maryland, Missouri, Montana, Nebraska, Nevada, New Hampshire, New Jersey, New Mexico, New York, North Carolina, North Dakota, South Carolina, Tennessee, Texas, and Wyoming) have filed or are in the process of filing lawsuits for the lack of adequate funding (Kennedy 2005). The crowded court dockets demonstrate the immediate need for school finance reform at the national level. Many state legislators adopt a reform strategy that temporarily increases funding. After a few years, however, legislators often fail to maintain the appropriate level of funding or increase the level of funding as they increase the responsibilities of the schools by raising "standards." Examples of this scenario can be found in new cases involving Kentucky, Idaho, and New Jersey where settlements in past lawsuits are no longer adequate (Kennedy 2005).

"The wheels of justice turn slowly" is an apt cliché for many school finance lawsuits. In 1993, the Idaho Supreme Court ruled that the state's school finance system was unconstitutional. The case was reviewed, re-reviewed, and finally settled in 2006. Similarly, New York City has been engaged in a twelve-year battle for financial equity in public school funding with the State of New York. After 12 years, the Campaign for Fiscal Equity has won its case and has reported that New York City schools will receive $9.2 billion over five years for capital improvements. In addition, the state needs to supply New York City over four years with $5.63 billion in additional operating funds (Kennedy 2005, 1).

New York is not a lone case. In 1972, the New Jersey school funding statute was ruled unconstitutional. The New Jersey Supreme Court found that the funding of schools "violated the thorough and efficient clause of the state constitution, as well as the equal protection clause of the U.S. Constitution" (Morley 1997). Again in 2002, after a dozen or more finance opinions by the New Jersey Supreme Court, the State of New Jersey was ordered to work out a plan to provide additional equity to 30 of its poorest districts. The state issued $8.6 billion in bonds, of which $6 billion was for construction and renovation in these 30 districts (National Access Network 2006; Kennedy 2005).

According to the Educational Priorities Panel report (2000), Dr. David Armor, a "part-time researcher at George Mason University" said, "School resources have virtually no effect—very, very little effect on student achievement." The report also notes that Dr. Eric Hanushek of the University of Rochester argued that "money has no significant impact on student achievement" and that "there is no relationship between smaller class size, teacher quality and student performance." Some attorneys for New York State argued that an eighth-grade education is sufficient (Sanders 2005). This flies in the face of those who want the United States to compete in a global market. Krugman (2005) reported on the Toyota Motor Company's moving from the southern United States to Canada. The reason given was that "trainers for the Japanese plants in Alabama had to use pictorials to teach illiterate workers how to use high tech equipment" (A23). The city of New York does not have vehicle assembly plants within city limits, but we are certain that one of the major financial centers of the world requires a workforce with a level of education beyond the eighth grade. We acknowledge that money alone does not equate to high levels of achievement, but even the most tightfisted politician cannot deny that children in safe, well-funded schools usually perform better on academic tasks than children of poverty who attend crowded, dangerous schools with few instructional resources or opportunities.

In a study of the schools on Long Island in New York, researchers found significant relationships among the general wealth of the surrounding school community, the length of time that students had been in poverty, and test achievement data (Johnson, Johnson, Farenga, and Ness 2005). The results support the findings of Cohen (2000), who argues that "one of the oldest, most reliable findings in sociology of education is the relationship between socioeconomic status of the family, race, ethnicity, and academic achievement" (274).

Schools on Long Island cover small geographic regions when compared to schools in other parts of the country. It is not unusual for communities to have only two or three schools in a single district (e.g., East Rockaway Union Free School District [UFSD], East Williston UFSD, Floral Park-Bellerose UFSD, Quogue UFSD). Some districts are comprised of three school buildings ranging from kindergarten to grade 4, grades 5 to 8, and grades 9 to 12. Each of the schools has a full administrative staff of principal, assistant principals, and support staff. Then there is a central administration with a superintendent and assistant superintendents for business, curriculum, personnel, and transportation. What is even more unique to Long Island is that within a mile, or in some cases, within blocks, there is another independent school district, complete with a full house of administrative personnel. Economy of scale is lost on Long Island because most parents seem to want small school districts with local control.

We suggest that the real reason for such small districts is that many people do not want to integrate racially or economically. Long Island is a microcosm of several areas of the country where people are stratified into communities by their socioeconomic status. There are intradistrict discrepancies in educational funding and in the demographic makeup of the schools' populations—even in unified school districts that encompass more than one community. The trends of increased segregation, inequities in educational funding, greater levels of economic stratification, and the increased insulation of middle-class and upper-middle-class communities from poverty and minority populations is well documented (Berliner 2005; Boger, 2005; Borman, Eitle, Michael, Eitle, Lee, Johnson, Cobb-Roberts, Dorn, and Shircliffe 2004; Natriello, McDill, and Pallas 1990; Orfield and Lee 2005; Orfield, Bachmeier, James, and Eitle 1997). If local control were the primary reason for wanting small districts, people would have been more outraged with the cost and burden of mandated standards, overregulation, and cumbersome requirements being put on their districts by state and federal agencies. Perhaps individuals believe that they have control of their local schools because they vote on school district budgets. In reality, the only items that they generally vote on are maintenance, athletics, and some levels of transportation. Even when budgets are defeated, teacher and administrator salaries are not affected because they are contractual. It is no wonder that when original budgets are defeated and austerity budgets are put in place, the tax savings are so minimal. It is also no wonder that poorer communities defeat their budgets more often than their wealthier counterparts. The characteristics of these schools often reflect the community at large.

Teachers in Poor and Rich Schools

Teachers in poorly funded schools in different states were interviewed on a number of education issues. Karen Allen is a fourth-year high school teacher in a low-income New York community. There are 4,000 students who attend two separate high schools housed in the same building. Karen described some aspects of her school:

> One hundred percent of my students admit they have friends who belong to a gang. The school is 75 years old. Heat is sometimes a problem in the building. For example, I taught an entire week with no heat and it was horrible. The gym needs to be improved desperately. We do have a swimming pool, but it is being used as storage for old furniture. Since the budget has had problems over the last couple of years, supplies are very limited to teachers. If you request filing folders you will only receive 10 at a time. We don't have a lot of maps in the social studies classrooms. We have a total of five copy machines in the building and they are always broken. Most importantly, we hardly have any paper available. We have one faculty room with a telephone, and it's hard to get to the phone during the day. It also very hard to get field trips approved because of the lack of money available.

Bobbie Blanchet is a middle school English teacher in a low socioeconomic, mostly minority town on Long Island. Some of her students are homeless. Bobbie said:

> Their home life is pretty bad—drugs, alcohol. Gangs are a big problem. It's not safe. I leave before it's dark. This is a rough place. For supplies I got a stapler, tape dispenser, about a dozen colored folders, one board eraser, a few pieces of chalk left from last year, a box of paper clips, three packs of computer paper. That's it. Our only field trip is to Petco and Pathmark [a supermarket], the stupidest and cheapest trips available. There are only two kinds of teachers here: great, amazing, change-the-future kind, and bad—can't-get-a-job-anywhere-else type.

Danelle Zenker, a first-grade teacher in a medium-sized east Texas city, is in a school that serves children who live in trailer parks, government housing, and multifamily homes. Seventy-six percent are eligible for free lunch. Danelle recounted:

> The home life of many of the students is unstable and dysfunctional. They are faced with fathers in prison, mothers working two jobs while an older sibling

takes care of them, living with grandparents, sleeping on mats, on the floor, or two or three to a bed. Some of the students tell how their electricity and water get turned off and then turned back on. Most of the students do not have a home telephone. I have several students that relate the abuse of their mother by their father to me. I have seen bruises and black eyes on mothers as they come up to the school. I have had to report four children for being abused by their parents.

Once a year a dental unit travels to the school and provides dental care for the students. It is in a RV-type trailer. Teachers are given a hundred dollars to buy teaching supplies. The teachers pay for other teaching supplies. I spend around $2,500 of my own money each year for supplies for my students.

Samantha Jones is an alternative high school teacher in New York City. She reported:

More than 85 percent of our students have not passed the English Language Assessment (ELA). Their English and reading skills are far below grade level. Trying to prepare the students for academic success is very difficult because they are having so many problems at home. We have students who have their own children. I am working with two students who are up for attempted murder. Their focus is far from schoolwork.

My class size varies. One has 40 students, another 38. There are about 15 textbooks for the two classes combined. Many pages are ripped out, there is gum in or on them, and they are above the students' reading levels. The other class I teach has 28 students. That class has no textbooks, so I am constantly making photocopies and handing out papers and folders.

The school has no nurse's office, no teachers' lounge, no library. The computer lab has 20 outdated, virus-embedded computers. That is our only technology. The computer room has one printer and students are not allowed to print out more than one page. I go to the public library and bring books into the school.

The security guards have to take away students' knives before they come into the building. Outbursts in classrooms and fighting are common. Yet, I am supposed to read a script on what and how to teach.

Every student gets a free breakfast and lunch and a Metro [subway] card. Teaching in a poor performing urban school is emotionally and physically draining. Most teachers here want the students to learn, but we have no support from the "powers that be." I have spent over $800 so far this year, and it is only November, on supplies and books for the classroom. Not only do we teach students but also critters such as the rat, mouse, and roach population. Some days they seem to pay more attention to me than the students.

Darlene Washington is a sixth-grade teacher in a small, wealthy school district on Long Island. She responded to a wide range of questions about her situation. The contrast between Darlene's school and the low-income schools is striking:

In this building students are overwhelmingly affluent. Some of my students have nannies and most of them have tutors to help with their school work. Very often you will see designer clothes; girls have designer handbags, Prada, Gucci, and such. You can tell it's a wealthy community. Vacations are occurring even when school is in session. I often hear of kids taking cruises, and they have second homes they visit.

The parents are wealthy enough to pay for activities but often the kids are overwhelmed with instrument lessons, acting lessons, sports, tutors. Over the summer, almost all the kids attend sleep-away camp. They have very busy little lives.

Well, I'm in the middle school, but it is close to the high school and you can see that the students there have much nicer cars than most of the teachers. All of the cars in the student parking lot are new and very expensive.

A majority of my students want to go to big-name colleges. They are talking about them now in sixth grade. There are a lot of gated communities. The houses vary in size, but most are large. Each teacher has a computer and a telephone with a main line out. There is a supply closet the teachers can go to whenever they need anything.

The eighth graders go to Washington, D.C. every year for their field trip. In sixth grade, we usually go to a Broadway show, and we visit the Vanderbilt Planetarium. Each grade has a guidance counselor. We have a school psychologist and a nurse with an assistant as well as administrators.

I do not think these kids are aware of poverty in the least. They are caring and giving, but I just think they are surrounded by wealth and they have never seen anything else. They do not understand that even two towns away there are kids who have nothing. To them, how they live is the norm.

Elvira Berk also teaches on Long Island. She stated:

One of the great things that teachers enjoy in my district is the access to technology. There are several computers with high-speed Internet connections in every classroom. In the two middle schools, all sixth graders are given a laptop that they use throughout the day.

Another great thing about my school district is that teachers don't need to spend their own money on things that they need. If we need supplies, all we have to do is fill out a supply request form, and then we are given whatever we need. If we want to go on a field trip, the district funds it without hesitation. We also never have to worry about our textbook supply because our students have a second copy of the texts for home use.

Jason Jordan, a middle school science teacher in an affluent New York City suburb explained:

Whenever I mention the Grand Canyon or other major geological formations in national parks, some of my students are quick to raise their hand and say, "I was there!" And this response is repeated for many areas of the country and abroad. They can readily bring in brochures, field guides, and park notes. Some examples that I've seen include "Point Reyes Peninsula and the San Andreas Fault Zone," "Point Reyes National Seashore Gray Whales," "Crater Lake [Oregon]: The Story behind the Scenery," and "The Ecology of the Everglades [Florida]."

These students have an advantage when complex topics such as animal migration, ecology, the law of superposition, evolution, and weathering are discussed in the life or earth sciences.

Mr. Jordan added:

> You can't miss the students who travel. They wear the experience like people wear jewelry. What I mean is that you can easily notice the athletes in the class, and you can just as easily notice the children who've had worldly experiences based on their travels. Their language, their outlook on the world, and the complexity of their thoughts all come to light during class discussions. The ease with which children share where they've been and what they've seen is apparent. Travel is an outstanding opportunity and education in itself. Substituting a week of school to visit Hong Kong, Paris, or Rome is no loss because of the education that's gained from the first-hand travel experience. Besides, most students have the option of working with a tutor to make up any work they've missed.

In New York, students of Karen Allen, Bobbie Blanchet, and Samantha Jones will take the same high-stakes tests as Darlene Washington's, Elvira Berk's, and Jason Jordan's students.

The ZIP Code Method

It is often said that the easiest and quickest way to estimate family income in nearly any community is by looking at the five-digit ZIP code. Coast to coast, these government postal codes provide reliable community data. On the West Coast, *92037* represents La Jolla, California, an affluent community that is part of San Diego's unified school district. The La Jolla schools have few commonalities with the rest of the San Diego school district. La Jolla Senior High School is the district's highest achiever on state tests, receives recognition in national competitions, and has obtained independence from the district's curriculum mandates (Tomsho 2006: A1). The La Jolla Senior High School's student body is 63.2 percent white, 23.3 percent Hispanic, 10.1 percent Asian, 1.7 percent African American, and 1.7 percent "other." Approximately 18 percent of the students are eligible for free or reduced lunch (California Department of Education 2006b). The San Diego district's average is 53.5 percent eligible for free or reduced lunch. Hoover High School, where 58.8 percent qualify for free or reduced lunch, is represented by the ZIP code *92115*. The enrollment breakdown for Hoover High School is 64.7 percent Hispanic, 15.8 percent African American, 12.7 percent Indochinese, 4.4 percent white, 1 percent Asian, and 1.5 percent other (California Department of Education 2006a).

Test score comparisons between La Jolla Senior High School and Hoover Senior High School reveal significant differences. Using the Academic Performance Index (API) that measures schools throughout the state of California, on a scale from 2 to 1,000, La Jolla Senior High School achieved an 834 in 2005 and Hoover Senior High School achieved a 580. The API is calculated from state norm-referenced tests, the California Standards Test (CST), and the California High School Exit Examination (CAHSEE). California has set the statewide API goal at 800 and above.

On the East Coast, the ZIP code *11530* represents Garden City, New York. A review of test scores, academic achievement, percentage of students attending college, and the percentage of students who are eligible for free or reduced lunch parallels the data of La Jolla Senior High School nearly 3,000 miles away. Contiguous to Garden City's southern boundary is Hempstead, New York, which is represented by the ZIP code *11550*. The Hempstead school district is 65 percent black, 34 percent Hispanic, and less than 1 percent white, Asian, and American Indian (greatshools.net 2006). Approximately 64 percent of all students are eligible for free or reduced lunch (New York State Education Department 2006b). The data for Garden City reveal a different demographic picture. Ninety-six percent of the students are white non-Hispanic, 3 percent are Asian, and less than 1 percent are Hispanic and black (greatshools.net 2006). No (0 percent) students are eligible for free or reduced lunch (New York State Education Department 2006a). Postsecondary plans for each of the districts differ as well. In Hempstead, 32 percent of the students plan to attend a four-year college; in Garden City, 90 percent of the students plan to attend a four-year college.

The differences between the two communities are illustrated in a description by Applebome (2005, 25):

> In the Balkanized geography of Long Island, where you can almost feel the differences in temperature between the have and have-not towns, it's not hard to figure out which category Hempstead fits in. With its drab, dilapidated apartment buildings with names like House Beautiful, the rap and salsa pouring out of car windows downtown, Hempstead is a place where even the trees seem to instantly disappear as soon as you cross the border from affluent Garden City. . . . Its [Hempstead's] test scores are among the lowest on Long Island. The high school has had 11 principals since 1994.

The analyses make it evident that the communities of La Jolla, California and Garden City, New York, have more in common with each other than they do with their neighboring schools or districts within a closer proximity. They have high levels of achievement, similar levels of affluence, and similarities in race and ethnicity—the overwhelming majority being white. Achievement adheres to economic boundaries.

There are districts in which a range of socioeconomic statuses are represented in a single school. Tara Green is a Long Island middle school teacher in such a school. Tara said:

> The wealthy students all have designer clothing, bags, you name it. Everything is Prada, Bebe, Louis Vuitton—and these are middle-school children. The poor students, on the other hand, literally need sneakers and coats. They come to school with holes in their shoes and no jackets at all simply because they have outgrown their old coats and can't afford to buy new ones. The principals in my district hold coat drives throughout the different schools. Our school will hold one and then we'll switch our donations with another school so that we avoid a situation where one student donates a coat and then the next day the poor kid who sits next to him in math has the coat on. It seems to work.
>
> The wealthy kids have cell phones, BlackBerrys, and iPods. They also have debit cards on which their parents give them a certain limit each week or month. The new big thing is a mall gift card, and a lot of them use these instead of bringing money to the mall.
>
> The wealthy middle schoolers have been all over the world, from Asia to Europe to the Caribbean Islands. Some of them have vacationed more than once at Turks and Caicos, which is supposedly the "Beverly Hills" of the Caribbean. They travel all the time, during the summer, holiday breaks, you name it. The poor students don't travel at all. Some have never been out of New York State.
>
> The wealthy parents hire expensive private tutors for their children. They play sports on the town teams. They also attend summer camps for sports or the arts, depending on their interests. Some play musical instruments. Some of the poorer students qualify for camps that are paid for using fundraising money. Some of them play school-sponsored sports because it doesn't cost anything to play on a school team.

John Erickson is a teacher in a New York high school that is characterized by the diversity of its students, particularly in terms of family wealth. He noted:

> I don't think that kids with less money hang out with bad people or anything like that. But kids who do have money are usually very popular because they have the cool car and the nice clothes and the Gucci bags. And they have friends who play sports, friends who are thespians, and club friends. Everyone loves them. But it all has to do with the advantages they have. Of course the kids who have money play sports and play instruments. Their parents have the money to buy them the equipment. If you go to see a school play, you can see that most of the actors are kids who are spoiled rotten. You rarely have a star athlete whose family has nothing.

We have AP sciences, history, and languages at this school, and you have to pay to take the classes because you get college credit. Right off the bat, if your family doesn't have money to spend, you're not taking those classes.

Teaching and learning in schools such as Tara Green's and John Erickson's present their own challenges. It must be difficult for the students of poverty to rub shoulders, day after day, and to compete with children who have everything. The teachers must try to provide the background knowledge and experiences to some of their students that other students already have. This is not an easy task. Regardless of differences in family wealth or all of the other factors discussed in this book, students take the same high-stakes tests. Many won't graduate from high school because of a test or will have to repeat eighth grade because of a test. The deck is stacked against the less-affluent students who don't have the advantages of travel, Advanced Placement courses, and more.

School Funding Discrepancies

An examination of educational funding shows systematic discrepancies that favor the affluent in education throughout the United States. Unified school districts (e.g., San Diego), union free school districts (e.g., Garden City and Hempstead), and large or small districts exhibit a pattern of additional material benefits to communities which are already affluent (American Federation of Teachers 2006; Janofsky 2005; Winter 2004). Even within a unified school district, intraschool funding differences occur. The less fortunate school, which is usually the one with the highest concentration of poverty and minority students, receives fewer resources. In spite of federal and state policies, talk of higher standards and increased funding for education, schools in poor communities are shortchanged. A report on educational funding by government agencies prepared by the Education Trust-West (2005) states, "Instead of providing more resources to the schools and districts that serve concentrations of low-income and minority students, they provide less" (1). In California, the problem is particularly insidious. It demonstrates a reverse Robin Hood scenario, where government policies take away from those in need and reward those who have. "First we spend less in the districts in which poor and minority students are concentrated. Then we make matters worse by spending significantly less on the schools within those districts that serve [these] students" (1).

There are two kinds of differences that exist when we investigate issues of equity. The most apparent differences between poor schools and affluent schools are the visible structures of the physical plant (i.e., the school buildings). Martin Luther King Jr. Middle School in Monroe, Louisiana, for example, has so much standing water underneath the school's foundation that fish can be seen in the water. Principal Debbie Blue said, "There needs to be a way to pump water out from under the building, because, during mosquito time we have mosquitoes and lots of bugs" (Blum 2006). The school district's maintenance manager stated that he would not send his workers under the structure because when it rained the water was too deep.

Other resources, such as updated textbooks, computers, sports facilities, and libraries, also reveal inequities in education funding. In addition to these, there are the hidden gaps. Items such as differences in teacher salaries, teacher qualifications and experience, the number of educators teaching within their certification area, and overcrowded classrooms have a cumulative impact on education. Further, high-poverty, high-minority schools are unevenly staffed in the support services provided by educational specialists, counselors, social workers, and psychologists. *Rodriguez v. Los Angeles Unified School District* sought to remedy these inequities in school resources. In 1992, an agreement was reached that required the Los Angeles Unified School District to move toward equal per pupil expenditures. Since that time, however, the decree has been dissolved. In an attempt to address needs of poor and minority students, the State of California has approved legislation to devote "as much as" $1 billion to repair deteriorating schools, $50 million for needs assessments, and $139 million to update textbooks (California Teachers Association 2006). Prior to this allocation, California ranked 44th in the nation for per pupil spending (Education Trust-West 2005, 2). The real issues of equity go beyond the line items in a school budget and include decisions about how the monies filter down to benefit those in need.

The nature versus nurture debate has been argued since antiquity. It is clear to many, however, that genes that have potential require an environment of expression. "It takes a village to raise a child" is a well-worn proverb. But what happens when the economic, educational, and social resources of a village are wanting? What happens when communities are so impoverished that basic services and career opportunities are limited to only a lucky few? To be raised in these communities, one finds little to supplement his or her formal education. Many models have been created that have examined the issue of education equity. The models have focused on schools, teachers, and students but most have failed to address the basic issue of poverty and the effects of poverty on a child's early development.

Popham (1998, 7) states:

> If you want to predict how well a school's students will score on a standardized achievement test, simply find out what the average parental income is for that school. If parental income is high, students will usually score well. If parental income is low, anticipate lower scores. Students in schools serving advantaged families will almost always get high standardized test scores; students in schools serving disadvantaged families will almost always get low standardized test scores.

A study of the relationship between poverty and the genetic expression of intelligence was conducted by Turkheimer, Haley, Waldron, D'Onofrio, and Gottesman (2003). The researchers found evidence that genes are influenced by social class. That is, social class provides the opportunity for genetic expression. Duncan and Brooks-Gunn (2001) demonstrated that changes in environmental conditions may have the greatest positive impact on the poorest children. Berliner (2005) summarizes these phenomena by arguing that "the simplest explanation available is that poverty and all that it entails, causes a restriction in genetic variation in intelligence" (971). If schools could return to instruction that provides experiential learning and enrichment instead of the current test-preparation curriculum, children of poverty could be helped rather than punished.

The present method of funding education in the United States raises questions of equity and the need for corrective justice. In all states except Hawaii, education is paid for in some measure by local property taxes. This has created a system of de facto economic determinism. Districts with economic wealth as measured by their tax base have less of a problem in raising the needed funds to support their share of the cost of educating America's youth. Poorer districts that have low levels of revenue generally have proportionately higher taxes to compensate for depressed property values. The tax burden causes even greater stress on people living in these communities. Legislators in many parts of the country have responded to these inequities by devising a plan to guarantee all schools a base amount of revenue on a per-pupil basis. Such policies, however, further the inequities in educational funding. Affluent districts add their healthy property tax revenues to the across-the-board state revenues and end up with a lot of money they can spend on education. Poor districts, on the other hand, must rely heavily on the state allocation because of their limited tax base. Providing equal per-pupil amounts to poor and affluent school districts only exacerbates and perpetuates the educational discrepancies.

Rothstein's (2004) *Class and Schools* provided ample evidence to link individual poverty, community poverty, race, and inequality in education. Boger (2005) found that the greatest achievement test gains by low-income students occurred when they attended middle-income schools. Similar results were found by Borman et al. (2004) who reported that black students who attended racially segregated schools performed more poorly on Florida state tests than black students who attended integrated schools. Duncan and Brooks-Gunn (2001) demonstrated that class size, early childhood intervention, and summer programs have the largest effect on the poorest of children. The literature is replete with evidence to support the position that creating an equitable environment for all does matter. It is clear that we have developed two school systems in the United States based on socioeconomic status: one system bestows numerous educational benefits, such as prekindergarten, art, music, science laboratories, and more on children. The other system offers no electives and plenty of mindless, lock-step test preparation to raise achievement scores. The deck is stacked against the excluded class and other children of poverty who are judged on the same high-stakes tests as children of privilege. Until corrective justice has been established, we encourage readers who are in agreement with the premise of this volume to make their feelings known at the ballot box.

References

Alexander, K., and M. D. Alexander. 1984. *The law of schools, students, and teachers.* St. Paul, MN: West Publishing.

American Federation of Teachers (AFT). 2006. Funding gap persists between rich and poor school districts. *American Teacher* 90 (7): 6.

Ancheta, A. 2004. Constitutional law and race-conscious policies in K–12 education. *ERIC Digest.* www.ericdigests.org/2003-2/race.html (accessed July 13, 2006).

Applebome, P. 2005. A schoolyard brawl, but it's the adults who are fighting. *New York Times,* July 17, 25.

Berliner, D. C. 2005. Our impoverished view of educational reform. *Teachers College Record* 108 (6): 949–995.

Blum, J. 2006. Water plagues MLK Middle School. *Monroe (LA) News-Star,* September 20. www.thenewsstar.com/apps/pbcs.dll/frontpage (accessed September 20, 2006).

Boger, C. 2005. *The socioeconomic composition of the public schools: A crucial consideration in student assignment policy.* Chapel Hill, NC: Center for Civil Rights.

Borman, K. M., T. M. Eitle, D. Michael, D. J. Eitle, R. Lee, L. Johnson, D. Cobb-Roberts, S. Dorn, and B. Shircliffe. 2004. Accountability in a postdesegregation era: The continuing significance of racial segregation in Florida's schools. *American Educational Research Journal* 41 (3): 605–631.

California Department of Education. 2006a. School accountability report card (SARC): Short version for academic year 2004–2005—Hoover Senior High School (San Diego, California). studata.sandi.net/research/sarcs/2005-06/SARC338short.pdf. Accessed on June 29, 2006.

California Department of Education. 2006b. School accountability report card (SARC): Short version for academic year 2004–2005—La Jolla Senior High School (La Jolla, California). ed-data.k12.ca.us/profile.asp?tab=1&level=07&ReportNumber=16&County=37&fyr=0405&District=68338&School=3733508. Accessed on June 29, 2006.

California Teachers Association. 2006. Real improvement may require changing how we fund schools. *California Educator* 10 (8). www.cta.org/CaliforniaEducator/v10i8/Feature_2.htm (accessed June 18, 2006).

Carr, M. 2005. School programs remain in limbo: Educators face slate of changes—again. *New Orleans Times-Picayune,* April 21. www.nola.live.advance.net/speced/nursinghomes/Thursday20050421/pdf (accessed April 21, 2005).

caselaw.findlaw.com. n.d. U.S. Supreme Court: *San Antonio School District v. Rodriguez* (1973). FindLaw. caselaw.lp.findlaw.com/scripts/getcase.pl?court=us&vol=411&invol=1 (accessed July 26, 2006).

Cohen, E. G. 2000. Equitable classrooms in a changing society. In *Handbook of the sociology of education*, ed. M. T. Hallinan, 265–283. New York: Kluwer.

Duncan, G. J., and J. Brooks-Gunn. 2001. Poverty, welfare reform, and children's achievement. In *Social class, poverty, and achievement*, ed. B. J. Biddle, 49–75. New York: Routledge Falmer.

Education Trust-West. 2005. *California's hidden teacher spending gap: How state and district budgeting practices shortchange poor and minority students and their schools.* Oakland, CA: Author.

Educational Priorities Panel. 2000. State's shameful defense: Money doesn't matter. *EPP Monitor* 4 (2). www.edpriorities.org/Pubs/PubsArchive/pubs_00Sum.Mone.html (accessed June 18, 2006).

———. 2001. Pataki stalls CFE victory. www.edpriorities.org/Info/StateFunEqui/info_StateFun.CFEAppel.html (accessed July 26, 2006).

Hempstead School District, Hempstead, New York. 2006. www.greatschools.net (accessed July 23, 2006).

Janofsky, M. 2005. Federal spending increases, but more schools will get less money for low-income students. *New York Times,* July 4, A9.

Johnson, D. D., and B. Johnson. 2006. *High stakes: Poverty, testing, and failure in American schools,* 2nd ed. Lanham, MD: Rowman & Littlefield.

Johnson, D. D., B. Johnson, S. Farenga, and D. Ness. 2005. *Trivializing teacher education: The accreditation squeeze.* Lanham, MD: Rowman & Littlefield.

Kantrowitz, B. and P. Wingert. 2006. What makes a high school great? *Newsweek,* May 8, 50–60.

Kennedy, M. 2005. Equity and adequacy. *American School and University,* May 1. www.asumag.com/mag/university_equity_adequacy/index.html (accessed June 18, 2006).

Klausnitzer, D. 2004. Rich school, poor school. *Tennessean.com,* May 9. www.tennessean.com/ education/archives/04/05/51062761.shtml (accessed June 19, 2006).

Klurfield, J. M. 2006. Beyond the ballot: Seven ways to ease the school tax pain. *Newsday,* May 14, A28.

Krugman, P. 2005. Toyota, moving northward. *New York Times,* July 25, A23.

La Morte, M. W. 1990. *School law: Cases and concepts.* 3rd ed. Englewood Cliffs, NJ: Prentice-Hall.

McGuire, K. 1990. Emerging issues in state-level school finance. *ERIC Digest.* www.ericdigests.org/pre-9217/finance.htm (accessed June 18, 2006).

Morley, M. 1997. Education for all—facing the challenges of New Jersey's public school system. Princeton University Law Journal, Fall. www.princeton.edu/~lawjourn/Fall97/III1morley.html (accessed July 26, 2006).

National Access Network. 2006. New Jersey. Project of the campaign for educational equity, Teachers College, Columbia University. www.schoolfunding.info/states/nj/lit_nj.php3 (accessed June 25, 2006).

Natriello, G., E. L. McDill, and A. M. Pallas. 1990. *Schooling disadvantaged children: Racing against catastrophe.* New York: Teachers College Press.

Neville, J. 1986. *Constitutional law.* New York: Harcourt Brace Jovanovich.

New York State Education Department. 2006a. School report card data, 2004–2005: Garden City High School. emsc32.nysed.gov/repcrd2005/schools/280218030007.shtml (accessed June 29, 2006).

———. 2006b. School report card data, 2004–2005: Hempstead High School. emsc32.nysed.gov/repcrd2005/schools/280201030007.shtml (accessed June 29, 2006).

Orfield, G., M. D. Bachmeier, D. R. James, and T. Eitle. 1997. *Deepening segregation in American public schools.* Cambridge, MA: Harvard Project on School Desegregation.

Orfield, G., and C. M. Lee 2005. *Why segregation matters: Poverty and educational inequality.* Cambridge, MA: Civil Rights Project, Harvard University.

Popham, W. J. 1998. A message to parents: Don't judge your child's school by its standardized test scores. Paper presented at the annual meeting of the American Educational Research Association, San Diego, April 13–17.

roslyntaxpayer.com. 2006. Business as usual: Spend, spend, and then some! April 23. www.roslyntaxpayer.com/id6.html (accessed June 25, 2006).

Rothstein, R. 2004. *Class and schools: Using social, economic, and educational reform to close the black-white achievement gap.* New York: Economic Policy Institute.

San Diego City Schools. 2006a. School accountability report card (SARC): Short version for academic year 2004–2005: Hoover Senior High School (San Diego, California). studata.sandi.net/research/sarcs/2005-06/SARC338short.pdf (accessed June 29, 2006).

———. 2006b. School accountability report card (SARC): Short version for academic year 2004–2005: La Jolla Senior High School (La Jolla, California). studata.sandi .net/research/sarcs/2005-06/SARC342short.pdf (accessed June 29, 2006).

Sanders, S. 2005. Legislature rejects Pataki's education cuts, even as governor continues stalling on CFE. Education Update Online. April. www.educationupdate.com/ archives (accessed June 23, 2006).

Scheuer, J. 1999. Checkerboard schooling: How state aid affects high-minority school districts in New York State. Educational Priorities Panel. www.edpriorities.org/ Pubs/Report/Report_Checker.html (accessed June 25, 2006).

Tomsho, R. 2006. Textbook battle: Top high schools fight new science as overly simple— San Diego's physics overhaul makes classes accessible, spurs parental backlash—test scores barely budge. *Wall Street Journal,* April 13, A1.

Turkheimer, E., A. Haley, M. Waldron, B. D'Onofrio, and I. Gottesman. 2003. Socioeconomic status modifies hereditability of IQ in young children. *Psychological Science* 14 (6): 623–628.

U.S. Census Bureau. 2002. Profile of general demographic characteristics (Detroit, Michigan). censtats.census.gov/data/MI/1602622000.pdf (accessed June 28, 2006).

———. 2005. *Public education finances 2003.* Washington, DC: U.S. Census Bureau.

usinfo.state.gov. n.d. Introduction to the court opinion of the *Plessy v. Ferguson* case. www.usinfo.state.gov/usa/infousa/facts/democrac/33.htm (accessed July 26, 2006).

Winter, G. 2004. Financial gap is widening for rich and poor schools. *New York Times,* October 6, A19.

7

The Tutoring Industry

THE BUSINESS OF TUTORING HAS BEEN A STAPLE of education since early times. From recorded history to today, tutoring has been available for students (or apprentices) who could afford it. In the early Greek period, wealthy Athenian families would send their sons off to study with one of the many Sophist philosophers (such as Protagoras, Gorgias, Callicles) to learn the valuable skill of rhetoric for preparation to enter the prestigious fields of law and political service. During medieval and Renaissance times, children—usually boys—from privileged families were able to benefit and profit from the opportunities of learning from a private tutor who was often a monk or a male affiliated with the university. The convention of gender and social-class bias in one-on-one tutoring continued through the eighteenth and nineteenth centuries and even through the early twentieth century.

The Growth of Tutoring

Tutoring practices within the last decades have changed dramatically and have grown at a near-exponential rate. This has happened for a number of reasons. First, the growing high-stakes testing movement has impelled a number of parents, even those whose annual income is modest, to apportion household funds for their children's after-school tutoring to give them a better chance to pass "the test." In most of these situations, one-on-one tutoring or small-class after-school tutoring might just be what it takes for a student to gain that extra competitive edge to pass an important examination.

Second, the so-called age of accountability in which we now live has shifted state and federal resources toward education in a way that has prompted for-profit corporations and smaller entrepreneurial groups to benefit from state and federal funding. The George W. Bush administration's No Child Left Behind (NCLB) Act included a provision that requires schools, whose student test scores are considered "failing," to use federal funds to contract with tutoring firms to work with economically poor students. The authorization for this work stems from the federally funded compensatory education program known as Title I (formerly Chapter I), which is based on a section of Public Law 107-110 (and its predecessor, Public Law 103-382), "Improving the Academic Achievement of the Disadvantaged." This provision has expanded the "access" to tutoring services in an attempt to deal with the achievement gap between rich and poor students.

Tutoring corporations have benefited from NCLB because of the more than $2 billion in federal monies allocated to "failing" districts for private, for-profit tutoring businesses. The case of New York City can be used as an example. According to Fertig (2006), "The city [of New York] is paying $80 an hour for [a student with poor reading skills] to receive a compensatory education by taking classes at the Huntington Learning Center. She'll get 1,500 hours at a total cost of $120,000." How much money can be made from tutoring? Let's extrapolate by putting this example into perspective: If only 10 students receive similar amounts of tutoring such as the student mentioned above, the tutoring corporation potentially could take in $1.2 million. Burnett (2004) reported that four districts in the suburbs of Chicago had paid more than $1.12 million for private tutors. About 50 schools in 23 surrounding districts were required under NCLB to hire private tutors in 2005. Burnett writes, "Do the math, and it's easy to see why tutoring companies like Kaplan, Sylvan and Score! seem to be popping up like Starbucks throughout the suburbs and across the country" (1). Burnett points out that many private, for-profit companies will not tutor certain populations including disabled students and pupils for whom English is a second language.

Third, with the advent of the Internet and other forms of global technology—chatrooms, discussion boards, weblogs and the like—for-profit, one-on-one, and small-class tutoring has become one of the fastest growing business sectors internationally. Tutoring service conglomerates, such as Kumon or Educate (Sylvan Learning), have become major players in the international tutoring scene. As a result of its early economic success in Japan, Kumon is present in more than 40 additional countries including the United States and Canada. Sylvan Learning began as a "Main Street" tutoring service in the outskirts of Los Angeles. Sylvan has grown into one of the leading tutoring companies in the United States and Canada and participates in e-tutoring services throughout the world. Thus, international and national (or local) tutoring firms and businesses have benefited from in-house tutoring as well as distance learning e-tutoring via the Internet.

There are two broad functions of tutoring enterprises active in the United States. One function is college entrance exam preparation with enrichment tutoring that typically serves students of wealthy families or those families with enough extra dollars to afford tutors. This type of service is exemplified by Eliot Shrefer, a Harvard graduate who became an SAT tutor in New York City. He spent three years tutoring Manhattan's richest youth so they could pass college entrance exams—including the SAT. Families paid up to $25,000 for tutoring services (Tyre 2006). The second major type of tutoring enterprise is found in the flourishing industry that focuses on elementary, middle school, and high schools designated as "failing" under NCLB dictates. Poor children in failing schools receive free tutoring under the law. The primary function of this type of tutoring is test preparation for high-stakes tests. In contrast to Shrefer with a degree from Harvard, who tutors SAT students, the NCLB-financed tutors and tutoring firms are a mixed bag. The billions in federal cash suddenly available for tutoring has led to a gold rush in the field, and not much is known about many of the tutors and their preparation for the task.

Problems with Tutoring Firms

Gootman (2006) reported on a New York City investigation of tutoring companies with which the city has contracts. Richard J. Condon, Special Commissioner of Investigation for the school system, issued a report on the findings. Two tutoring firms in particular came under fire. According to Gootman:

> Mr. Condon said one of his most disturbing findings was that the tutoring companies had failed to check employees' backgrounds, in some cases because of holes in City Education Department rules that have since been tightened. After fingerprints were checked, he wrote, it was determined that several Platform employees had been arrested for crimes including attempted murder and the sale of drugs, and that several Newton employees had been arrested for crimes including robbery and the criminal sale of a controlled substance. (B6)

The situation in New York City is not unique. The Chicago public school district has canceled its contract with Platform Learning in seven schools, claiming "the company is hurting children promised help under federal reforms" (Ohanian 2006, 1). Eleven hundred students were enrolled in tutoring in these seven schools. Platform Learning had contracted to provide tutoring to 14,000 children in 76 Chicago schools for $15 million. In Chicago, Platform

128 Chapter 7

tutors and substitute tutors didn't show up after school at one site, so the children watched a Garfield movie.

Several questionable and unethical tactics were used by tutoring firms in New York. These include:

- inappropriately recruiting students at their homes for tutoring
- offering principals $5,000 donations to their schools if they signed up 150 or more students
- offering a principal a trip to Puerto Rico
- offering students "gift certificates, CD players, and tickets to sporting events" (Gootman 2006, B1)

Some school employees "improperly gave tutoring companies confidential information about schoolchildren, including phone numbers and addresses, which the company used to track down prospective students" (B1).

Representative George Miller (D-California), member of the House Education and the Workforce Committee, issued a statement that expressed his concerns about aspects of the NCLB Act:

I am very concerned about reports of inducements—such as parents being given free computers, discount coupons, or signing bonuses—in exchange for selecting certain providers for their children. Suede-shoe operators are coming out of the woodwork and, in some cases, preying on parents and putting undue and inappropriate pressure on them to select providers that may not be the most qualified or the best suited to tutor their children. I am concerned . . . that all too often parents are being offered providers that are not necessarily effective or appropriate, because states do not live up to their monitoring and oversight responsibilities. (Miller 2005)

Murray (2005a, 1) explains:

Countless salespeople have been dispatched to school communities from coast to coast in hopes of wooing parents and eligible students with incentives ranging from cash prizes to basketball tickets. But as the competition for tutoring dollars heats up across the country, some industry watchers question whether SES [Supplemental Educational Services] might soon be headed the way of another multibillion-dollar school funding initiative that has taken recent heat for fraud, waste, and abuse: the eRate.

A company always has to be concerned about the bottom line—profit—or they go out of business. It is no wonder that there is a tutoring stampede mentality in New York City and elsewhere. During the school year ending in 2005, the school district paid tutoring companies a whopping $74.3 million (Gootman 2006).

The one-size-fits-all mentality of NCLB and the tutoring it has spawned flies in the face of all that we know about culture and human development. One principal, Carlos Azcoitia, said, "We saw they weren't really meeting the children's needs, and parents started to question if they were learning anything. They are not equipped to deal with English-language learners. There are constant classroom management issues" (Ohanian 2006, 2). Reynolds (2005) reports grave concerns about the quality of tutoring provided to American Indian children. He cites testimony to Congress from Dave Beaulieu, president of the National Indian Education Association. Beaulieu said, "The requirements of the statute [NCLB] and its timeframe for results do not recognize that schools educating Native students have an inadequate level of resources to allow for the effective development of programs known to work with Native students." A teacher at Rocky Boys in Montana, Bobby Ann Starns, pointed out, "NCLB emphasizes failure. . . . Native American needs are at one end of a continuum, and NCLB exists at another." Reynolds paraphrases Starns's comments:

> The law emphasizes the opposite of what is known about Native learning styles—that is, it rewards part-to-whole instead of whole-to-part learning, abstract thought instead of hands-on experience, and linguistic instead of visual teaching strategies. Starns characterized NCLB as ineffective and disrespectful of Native culture, a product of putative "scientific research" that is no more than the established opinion of a small group of influential non-Indians.

If the tutoring being provided by the for-profit firms disregards Native American culture and learning styles, surely the same could be said for other groups of minority children.

Some American citizens are concerned that their hard-earned tax dollars now are being sent to out-of-the-country online tutors. A big player in the international tutoring business is India. Das and Paulson (2005, 2) write: "Career Launcher is one of just five Indian firms currently tutoring U.S. students. Some contract with American e-tutoring providers, and some work directly with schools and students. Mr. Phadke [an official at Career Launcher] estimates that Indian tutors are now working with some 20,000 American students, but he hopes the market will increase as technology improves and demand from NCLB rises."

Although India may provide some fine tutors, we question why tax dollars are being sent to India when there are ample certified and retired teachers in poor children's neighborhoods who would be willing to tutor if permitted.

Oversight of Private Tutors

The U.S. Department of Education, under Secretary of Education Margaret Spellings, had forbidden school districts to use federal money to employ its own teachers as after-school tutors. Licensed, certified teachers had been barred from tutoring while for-profit tutoring entrepreneurs were free to hire whomever they wanted. Under pressure from some school district administrators, Spellings granted waivers to the urban school districts of Boston, Chicago, and New York City and four school districts in Virginia. In Florida, according to Murray (2005b), the state education department backed away from its plan to allow teachers to serve as tutors "amid complaints from private tutoring firms and direction from federal officials." Superintendent Thomas Payzant of the Boston Public Schools (BPS) notes that "in-house tutoring will cost BPS about $1,000 per student to provide 92 hours of tutoring compared to a cost of about $2,300 per student for 30–50 hours of private tutoring" (National School Boards Association 2005, 1). The waivers enabled the district to use their own teachers as tutors; however, conditions were imposed on the districts. These included having an independent evaluation of the tutoring program, filing a report at the end of the year, and making certain that private tutoring firms had "good access to the schools" (National School Boards Association 2005, 1).

The foolish nature of policies that give vast amounts of money to private tutors, some of whom may be unqualified, but deny the right to tutor to certified teachers who know their students and their community, is exacerbated by its support from important Washington politicians. John Boehner (R-Ohio), former chair of the House Committee on Education and House Majority Leader is on record stating:

> School districts identified as underachieving through the No Child Left Behind Act shouldn't be allowed to provide remedial tutoring to the students they are in danger of leaving behind. To do so would make a mockery of the entire Act. And the children in those schools deserve better. The tutoring options made available through No Child Left Behind are meant to provide a supplement for the questionable education those children are receiving from their public schools—not an expansion of that questionable education. Republicans agree private tutoring providers should be held to high standards, but ensuring federal tutoring funds are spent responsibly starts with ensuring underachieving public school districts are not eligible for those funds. My hope is that Secretary Spellings and the Education Department will continue to make clear that if a district isn't getting the job done with federal dollars in the classroom for children, it won't be entrusted with the responsibility of using federal dollars to provide tutoring for children either. (U.S. House Education and the Workforce Committee 2005, 1)

Boehner's apparent disdain for public school teachers' abilities is disheartening. He seems to be unaware of or unconcerned about the lack of documentation that the for-profit tutors are in any way prepared to deliver effective tutoring. The authors of this book would bet our money every time on certified, neighborhood classroom teachers rather than off-the-street hires, some of whom have not been screened. Most tutoring firms advertise that their tutors have been trained. But what type of training were they provided? Who did the training? What were the trainers' qualifications? What was the duration of the training? What were the minimum requirements to be hired as a tutor?

As of this writing, there seems to be no quality control imposed on the tutoring industry. A major flaw in NCLB requirements related to tutoring is that there is no mechanism to hold tutors and their employing firms accountable for results. Tutoring companies have not been required to demonstrate improvement on test performance by the children and youth they tutor. School teachers and administrators are held accountable, but for-profit tutoring corporations are not. It is likely that millions of dollars are being wrongly spent on an unproven giveaway. Saulny (2006, 38) states, "Even for those students who are getting tutored, there has yet to be a scientific national study judging whether students in failing schools are receiving any academic benefit. And there is no consensus on how that progress would be judged."

How are districts guaranteeing the quality of the outside tutoring agencies? At present, there are no standard credentialing requirements for becoming a tutor. Some providers assert that their tutors are "credentialed" which can mean anything from receiving in-house training from the tutoring center itself, receiving a high score on a standardized test, having some college preparation, or being a state-licensed professional in the field in which one is tutoring. Wise policy decisions would direct all these tutoring allocations to public school classrooms to be used for enriched education made possible by increased instructional resources, educational field trips, smaller class sizes, additional teaching assistants, targeted special development of teachers and staff, and a shift in policy that recognizes and addresses individual differences among learners.

By the end of 2006, several tutoring firms reported problems. Platform Learning filed for Chapter 11 bankruptcy protection, although it continued to provide tutoring in New York City and elsewhere (Borja 2006). Some firms had waning enthusiasm for providing tutoring because "they encountered such obstacles as district reluctance to permit companies to provide tutoring on school grounds, lack of communication between districts and parents about the tutoring programs, and what the companies see as bureaucratic red tape" (5). The companies also complained that they had difficulties getting students to attend the tutoring sessions. We welcome these corporations to the world of what schools must deal with on a daily basis—and then be "failed" for these circumstances that are out of their control.

Tutoring and Enrichment from an International Perspective

The current body of research on the subject of tutoring and enrichment is sparse. Nevertheless, nearly all studies seem to agree that the business and workaday affairs of the tutoring industry have changed drastically within the past three decades. Tutoring and test-preparation practices have grown at a brisk pace, not only in the United States, but throughout the world (Grimshaw 2005; Lim 2005; Miron 2005; Saulny 2005). In East Asian countries such as Japan and Taiwan, tutoring services known as "cram schools" serve as popular havens for students, especially students in high school, at the end of the school day. According to Goya (1993), most public high school students in Japan would fail college entrance examinations if it were not for the Japanese cram school referred to as *juku*. For a modest fee, students can obtain the services of cram schools primarily for the purpose of short-term test preparation with the occasional long-term educational goals as well. Moreover, cram schools are becoming increasingly popular in American cities such as New York and Los Angeles, especially those with a large number of immigrants from East Asian countries. The cram school, as a general growing business sector phenomenon, is also becoming popularized in the United Kingdom, where it is referred to as the "crammer."

Aside from the cram school trend, the middle- (one to six months of tutoring service) to long-term (over six months) tutoring service industry is a growing phenomenon in most postindustrialized countries. These include Canada, countries in Northern and Western Europe, Australia and New Zealand, and countries of the Pacific Rim. In Canada, urban areas experienced anywhere from 200 percent to 500 percent increases in the number of tutoring centers during the 1990s (Davies 2001). Lee (2005) writes that households in South Korea spent approximately $7.88 billion dollars (7.96 trillion Korean won) on private tutoring expenses that accounted for 34.1 percent of the average household budget in 2004.

Private tutoring also is becoming widespread in other countries throughout the world. The ratio of tutoring services to secondary schools in Turkey, for example, is nearly 1 to 1 (2,100 tutoring agencies to 2,500 secondary schools) (Tansel and Bircan 2002). In Egypt, although private, for-profit tutoring is not permitted by the Ministry of Education, it is one of the country's fastest-growing industries. For-profit tutoring businesses in Egypt often engage in unjust practices such as tutor tax evasion and a statistically significant contrast in tutoring benefits favoring males over females (Assaad and Elbadawy 2004). Not surprisingly, the tutoring industry plays a minimal role in developing countries, particularly in countries of South America, Africa, and Asia.

The lack of tutoring opportunities for children and students based on race and class seems to be a world-wide phenomenon. Bray (2003) conducted an international study on the adverse effects of tutoring and the role of national governments in promulgating the private tutoring industry. Bray points out how the effects of private tutoring corrupt the goals of education, for example, by giving help with homework assignments and teaching directly to the test. He reports that clients, almost entirely from upper-income households, become more disenchanted with school because oftentimes answers to questions are provided by the tutors and tutoring firms. He found this to be the norm in the five cases he had examined—Mauritius, Hong Kong, Republic of Korea, Singapore, and Taiwan.

Tutoring is an expanding $4 billion business in the United States (Miron 2005). More than 1,500 tutoring providers have been approved by state bureaucracies to provide tutoring geared toward passing high-stakes tests. Among these providers are 23 major, for-profit corporations (Johnson and Johnson 2006). These include Huntington Learning Centers, Kaplan K–12 Learning Services, Plato Learning Inc., the Princeton Review Inc., Platform Learning, and Sylvan Learning. Others providing tutoring are smaller nonprofit groups including the Boys and Girls Club of America and the YMCA.

All Tutoring Practices Are Not the Same

According to a recent NCLB press release, there were 2 million school-aged children who were eligible for free tutoring services under Title I (U.S. Department of Education 2006). But if 2 million school-aged children in the United States were eligible, then 11 million of the 13 million children under the age of 18 who live in households below the poverty line (U.S. Census Bureau 2004) were not.

Are elementary, middle, and high school students clamoring for the free tutoring available to them from taxpayer-paid private providers? Apparently not, according to a report by Saulny (2006). She found that only about 12 percent (226,000) of the approximately 2 million children who qualify for free tutoring under NCLB participated in tutoring in 2005. The percentages ranged from 10 percent (5,000 of 50,000 eligible) in Louisiana to about a quarter of those eligible in Maryland and just under half of those eligible in New York. With more than $1,800 per child of Title I money available for corporate tutoring, aggressive marketing strategies have been pervasive. So, why aren't more eligible students being tutored? Is it because the tutoring is not engaging or helpful? Is transportation a problem? Does the necessity of student after-school employment rule out tutoring for youth of poverty? Are the students burned out by so much test preparation during the regular school day that they don't have the wherewithal to withstand more test prep after school or during the summer? These are questions that have not been answered.

In affluent communities, tutoring is seen as a status symbol. Students attend highly competitive schools that offer a variety of electives and challenging programs. Those who attend such schools often have the option to self-select courses that were not recommended by teachers or guidance counselors. Students who have difficulties with a course of study have tutoring as an option. It is not unusual to hear students say, "I have an appointment with my tutor after school" or request that their parents find them a tutor. The students are generally being tutored for advanced placement (AP) subjects, achievement tests (SAT II), college admissions tests (SAT/ACT), a second foreign language, or mentoring in the arts. It is not uncommon for the tutoring centers that cater to this clientele to charge in excess of $100 per hour for services rendered. And a large number of these students receive more than one hour of tutoring a week. So, for example, a client whose children are tutored for two hours per week for 26 weeks of the school year will remit as much as $5,200 in tuition for after-school supplemental education per year for each child in a family.

There remains a single factor that has been a constant since early times: children from poor families have been excluded from either accessing or benefiting from solid, enrichment-style tutoring. Although the tutoring industry in the United States has surpassed the $4 billion mark, including more than $2 billion from NCLB (Miron 2005), children from poor families or whose family incomes are below the poverty line rarely receive strong tutoring services. Instead they get only test-preparation drills unlike the tutoring described next.

The Case of Ellis

Ellis is a 10th-grade student who lives in the suburbs of a large urban metropolitan area. As an only child from an affluent household, Ellis is afforded numerous amenities, one of which is tutoring service. Ellis enjoys the benefits of tutoring for both short- and long-term end. The short-term benefits include working with a tutor for test preparation whenever a subject test in school is being administered. The long-term benefits include weekly enrichment in four subjects: mathematics, chemistry, English literature, and ancient history.

Ellis's tutor, Ms. Howard, is a 58-year-old state-certified mathematics teacher who has won a number of distinguished awards for her content knowledge in mathematics and her pedagogical skill as a teacher. Ms. Howard earned her baccalaureate degree at a well-known Ivy League university majoring in biology and mathematics. Upon graduation, Ms. Howard enjoyed a 20-year career as a head associate for a large-sized pharmaceutical company. By the time she was 42, Ms. Howard decided on a career change—one in which she could have the opportunity to make a difference in young people's lives. She then became a secondary school teacher with expertise in life sciences and mathematics. She is current in her fields as evidenced by her membership in three professional organizations and her collaboration as an author of a number of articles in the fields of mathematics and the natural sciences. Ellis's parents pay the tutoring service $95 for each hour of tutoring. The tutoring service remunerates Ms. Howard with a wage of $45 per hour of tutoring services.

The following discourse between Ellis and his tutor is illustrative in terms of tutoring practices as a form of enrichment and indicative of the tutoring environment experienced by many upper-middle and upper-class students. The topic discussed is the area of polygons. The tutor presents a polygon and asks Ellis to systematically determine its area in terms of square units.

Ms. Howard: For most students, it's really difficult to solve a problem like this one. But do you think you know how to find the area of this geometric figure? If so, how would you go about solving it?

Ellis: Not really. I think I know the basics. Like, the idea that the size of the smallest square is equal to one square unit.

Ms. Howard: That's absolutely right, Ellis. Now let's take this a step further. If you cut any rectangle—now this of course includes squares, since a square is one kind of rectangle—that is, bisect any rectangle by drawing a diagonal from one corner, let's say the upper left corner to the bottom right corner, you then create two equal right triangles, the areas of which are half of the original rectangle. So, if I draw a rectangle made of two square units, each right triangle that is created from a diagonal drawn is equal to one square unit. If I draw a rectangle made of three square units, each right triangle that is created from a diagonal drawn is equal now to one and one-half square units. A diagonal drawn through a four square unit rectangle will produce a pair of two square unit triangles and so on.

Ellis: Yes I get it. That makes sense.

Ms. Howard: Now let me draw a figure, and I'd like you to tell me the area of this figure. Ready?

Ellis: Yup.

Ellis takes approximately three minutes to solve the problem.

Ellis: OK, I'm done.

Ms. Howard: Great. What did you get as the area to this geometric figure?

Ellis: I got 7.5 as an answer.

Ms. Howard: And how did you get that?

Ellis: Well, I counted all the full unit squares in the figure and counted 4 altogether. That leaves 3.5 units left.

Ms. Howard: So far, so good. What's next?

Ellis: I then realized that a diagonal of a rectangle that's two square units divides the rectangle into two right triangles each of which is equal to one square unit. There are two of those. So now we're up to an area of six, since four plus two equals six.

Ms. Howard: Wonderful. And the remaining 1.5? How did you get that?

Ellis: Well, there are three half units left for a total of 7.5.

Ms. Howard: You got it, Ellis.

One might wonder why events in this tutor-tutee dialogue demonstrate what we refer to as an optimal tutoring environment. First, we find that the content discussed in this one-on-one lesson is not presented in a rote, mechanistic manner, that is, as a list of facts that the student must memorize. Rather, the tutor presents the student with a problem that elicits knowledge of concepts through the identification of patterns and relationships. Engaging in mathematics this way allows the student to base an answer not on a memorized procedure or algorithm but on a systematic relationship between various concepts in geometry. For example, the method in which some teachers present the topic of the area of triangles is "Area is equal to one-half of the base times the height" ($A = \frac{1}{2} bh$). The method used by Ms. Howard, however, allows the student to learn the algorithm of a polygon through the conceptualization of certain patterns and relationships of quadrilaterals and the importance of diagonals—namely, that a diagonal bisects a rectangle into two congruent right triangles.

Second, the tutor's method for helping a student solve area problems allows for more flexibility in the ways in which the student thinks about particular mathematical ideas. It was often, and still is, the case that mathematical topics are taught in ways that present mathematical ideas in a static manner. Ms. Howard's presentation of the topic exhibits a more dynamic point of view through which concepts are presented deliberately with the use of a visual and tactile manipulative.

Third, although flexibility is mostly associated with activities that involve enrichment, it is a necessary factor that may contribute to successful test taking. For example, a question about the area of a geometric figure on an SAT examination might unnerve some students, who will either skip the question or spend five to ten minutes attempting unsuccessfully to solve it. Students must experience a flexible approach in order to successfully solve these and other types of mathematics problems. The general public, more than likely, did not learn the topic of area as a concept. Some teachers present procedures and algorithms in a rote way because they do not have the luxury of one-on-one time that someone such as Ms. Howard has.

Ms. Howard provides essential prompts and questions in leading Ellis not only to the correct answer, but to an understanding of the general concept inherent in the problem. This approach in teaching is more sensitive to the individual differences of learners than the standard teacher-centered approach, which may rely on little student input due to time constraints.

The Stacked Deck

The tutoring of Ellis is unlike that provided to students of the excluded class by businesses whose missions emphasize skill-and-drill, rote, test preparation exercises. Tutoring agencies that focus on this form of tutoring often use scripted lessons and procedures that need to be strictly followed. One Long Island tutor, Aaron Pulaski, who worked for a well-known for-profit tutoring corporation described his work:

> It was a very structured atmosphere where everyone was given a recipe based on the results of a student's achievement test. We taught to the test and moved through different levels: Books 1, 2, and 3. The director would speak to the parents. I was not permitted to speak to parents without a supervisor. They [the company] said it was to protect me. We had one week of training, between six and 12 hours, and were given a handbook of policies. It told how to follow a prescription, where to get books, and how to handle children who are constantly getting out of their chairs. It's an assembly-line mentality, and the students who are having trouble completing the assigned work from school are now being given an additional two hours of work a week to complete.

This method of tutoring is highly decontextualized, and students need only recognize an answer to a question in a mechanistic and associative manner rather than understanding the general rules and principles of a particular problem to be applied to later situations in different contexts. In addition, this tutoring style does not require a highly skilled instructor; one need only read or follow a script and provide the correct answers to questions.

In his 1971 book, *Beyond Freedom and Dignity*, psychologist B. F. Skinner served up perhaps one of the most telling and yet controversial accounts of how humans gain knowledge through learning and conduct their lives in the everyday context. One of Skinner's main arguments was that each individual human being eventually achieves a certain status in life, not because she possesses a particular genetic predisposition or is able to learn as a result of some a priori constructs of mind or cognition. Rather, Skinner says, the individual human being gets to where she is as a result of hundreds of thousands of positive and negative reinforcements that shape her behavior. Although we may speculate about the validity of Skinner's thesis (as Noam Chomsky [1967] did convincingly in his review of Skinner's *Verbal Behavior*), one major argument against the main thrust of the tutoring industry, namely, high-stakes test preparation, is that the main business of the test prep tutor is to "condition" the student with a modicum of reinforcements to pass the test—with or without content knowledge. In other words, the more one knows what the test makers are looking for, the greater the success rate of passing the test. One can learn how to pass a history test without knowing or learning much about history. Perhaps the most egregious problem is this: The more affluent the students' backgrounds, the more likely they are to benefit from expensive, private tutoring geared to their interests and the more likely the students will pass the test. The more impoverished the students are, the greater the likelihood of being assigned to uncredentialed tutors for a short time for drill and test-practice lessons in regimented sequence—and the greater the likelihood of failing the test. So even when children of poverty receive "free tutoring" through NCLB, the deck is stacked against them in terms of any genuine learning and enrichment. What differences in out-of-school activities are experienced by children of affluence and children of poverty? Chapter 8 examines these differences.

References

Assaad, R., and A. Elbadawy. 2004. Private and group tutoring in Egypt: Where is the gender inequality? Paper presented at the Annual Meetings of the Economic Research Forum, December 14.

Borja, R. R. 2006. Market for NCLB tutoring falls short of expectations. *Education Week*, December 20, 5, 13.

Bray, M. 2003. Adverse effects of private supplementary tutoring: Dimensions, implications, and government responses. Paris: International Institute for Educational Planning (UNESCO).

Burnett, S. 2004. Failing schools a windfall for private tutors. Students First Illinois, December 19. www.studentsfirst.us/printer/article.asp?c=136333 (accessed July 22, 2006).

Chomsky, N. 1967. A review of B. F. Skinner's *Verbal Behavior*. In *Readings in the psychology of language*, eds. L. A. Jakobovits and M. S. Miron, 142–143. Boston: Prentice-Hall.

Das, A., and A. Paulson. 2005. Need a tutor? Call India. *Christian Science Monitor*, May 23. www.csmonitor.com/2005/0523/p01s01-legn.htm (accessed July 9, 2006).

Davies, S. 2001. The rise of for-profit education: The case of private tutoring businesses. Paper presented to the Department of Sociology, University of Toronto, March 2001.

Fertig, B. 2006. Yamilka's Journey. *WNYC—New York Public Radio*, June 5. www.wnyc.org/news/articles/60848# (accessed June 6, 2006).

Gootman, E. 2006. Report assails tutoring firms in city schools. *New York Times*, March 8, B1, B6.

Goya, S. 1993. The secret of Japanese education. *Phi Delta Kappan*, 75 (2): 126–129.

Grimshaw, T. 2005. Tutoring boom. *ninemsn.com*, August 26. aca.ninemsn.com.au/stories/1928.asp (accessed June 9, 2006).

Johnson, D. D., and B. Johnson. 2006. *High stakes: Poverty, testing, and failure in American schools*, 2nd ed. Lanham, MD: Rowman & Littlefield.

Lee, H. S. 2005. Households' private tutoring costs reach w8 tril. in 2004. *Korea Times*, April 4. times.hankooki.com/1page/biz/200504 (accessed July 29, 2006).

Lim, S. 2005. Desire to lift kids gives tutoring market an "A": More parents increasingly spending money on private learning centers. *MSNBC.com*, August 5. www.msnbc.msn.com/id/8818220/ (accessed June 9, 2006).

Miller, G. 2005. Representative Miller statement on hearing on "Tutoring for children in underachieving schools." www.house.gov/apps/list/press/edlabor_dem/rel42605b.html (accessed March 24, 2007).

Miron, M. 2005. Tutoring industry growing rapidly. *Kalamazoo Gazette*, September 29. www.kzoo.edu/educ/reading_articles/tutoring_industry.pdf (accessed June 14, 2006).

Murray, C. 2005a. SES: Two billion reasons to worry. eSchool News, May 16. www.eschoolnews.com/news/showStory.cfm?ArticleID=5667 (accessed July 23, 2006).

———. 2005b. Feds tighten tutoring rules under NCLB. eSchoolNews, October 19. www.eschoolnews.com/news/showStory.cfm?ArticleID=5917 (accessed July 23, 2006).

National School Boards Association. 2005. Department of Education allows Boston Public Schools to provide tutoring. NSBA Cosa documents, November. www.nsba.org/site/doc_cosa.asp?TrackID=&SID=1&DID=37245&CID=164&VID=50 (accessed July 23, 2006).

Ohanian, S. 2006. NCLB outrages: Tutoring firm expelled from 7 of city's schools. SusanOhanian.org.susanohanian.org/show_nclb_outrages.html?id=1129 (accessed July 9, 2006).

Reynolds, J. 2005. Problems outweigh goals of No Child Left Behind. *Indian Country Today*, April 8. www.indiancountry.com/content.cfm?id=1096410717 (accessed July 9, 2006).

Saulny, S. 2005. A lucrative brand of tutoring grows unchecked. *New York Times*, April 4, A1, A18.

———. 2006. Tutor program offered by law is going unused. *New York Times*, February 12, 1, 38.

Skinner, B. F. 1971. *Beyond freedom and dignity*. New York: Knopf.

Tansel, A., and F. Bircan. 2002. Private tutoring expenditures in Turkey. Economic Research Forum Working Paper Series, Cairo.

Tyre, P. 2006. A Park Avenue tutor pens a tell-all. *Newsweek*, April 10, 54.

U.S. Census Bureau. 2004. Income stable, poverty up, numbers of Americans with and without health insurance rise, Census Bureau reports. U.S. Census Bureau News, August 26. www.census.gov/Press-Release/www/releases/archives/income_wealth/002484.html (accessed June 15, 2006).

U.S. Department of Education. 2006. Free tutoring under the No Child Left Behind Law. ED.gov Extra Credit newsletter, June 7. www.ed.gov/news/newsletters/extracredit/2006/06/0607.html (accessed June 15, 2006).

U.S. House Education and the Workforce Committee. 2005. Underachieving school districts shouldn't be eligible to offer federally funded tutoring, Boehner says. *News Update*, April 26, 1–3.

8

Life Experiences

IT SHOULD BE EVIDENT AT THIS POINT that the existence of chronic racism, poverty, violence, lack of health care, inequities of school funding, and questionable tutoring practices are major causes of low test scores. Poor children suffer from the consequences of economic segregation and the lack of vital services and financial resources. In addition, poor children have starkly different life experiences when compared to their more affluent counterparts. Children from middle- to upper-income households can expect to eat at least three somewhat well-balanced meals a day, but poor children often do not have this option. Moreover, children from middle- and upper-income households may have the opportunity to experience the world through travel and other related luxuries; most poor children do not have such benefits.

This chapter discusses differences in life experiences that provide affluent students with a competitive edge on high-stakes tests. The privilege that we discuss fits into two categories. The first category refers to privilege that is not earned but merely bestowed upon a person as a result of birthright. The second category of privilege refers to government policies or actions favoring a particular group. Some people are born into fortunate circumstances and often use their advantage to promote their own well-being. We have deep concerns with government policies that increase inequities. These are policies where "in twenty-five states, wealthier school districts had more state and local financing than did high poverty districts" (Winter 2004, A19). In addition to the widening financial gap for rich and poor schools (American Federation of Teachers [AFT] 2006), there have been practices and programs, such as the GI Bill of Rights and redevelopment plans separating the affluent from the poor, that fueled the rate of segregation and educational inequities by creating pockets of impoverished communities (Caro 1974; Davis 1990; Jacobs 1992; Picker 2002).

Government Policies and Community Development

Epstein and Saunders (2000) focused on the influence of environmental factors external from schools and institutions of higher education. The theory of overlapping spheres of community influence "integrates and extends several ecological, educational, psychological, and sociological perspectives on social organizations and relationships" (287). These overlapping spheres promote an opportunity for situated cognition, that is, thinking influenced by the environment in which it takes place. The basic element of the model is common responsibility for communication and respect among individuals and agencies involved in the community. The theory refocuses our attention to the interaction of family, school, and community from one of sequential development to one of simultaneous influences from childhood through adulthood. These overlapping spheres of influence contextualize James Coleman's (1988) concept of social capital. The more efficiently the community agencies function and interact, the greater the chance of increasing the social capital in the community. It is therefore critical to examine how certain communities are started, sustained, and transformed. The direct experiences learned in the community provide life lessons on equality, civic responsibility, democracy, and other forms of cultural literacy. This is the social capital that vibrant communities contain.

Stephen Ambrose, author and historian, stated that the "GI Bill was the best piece of legislation ever passed by Congress" (Lehrer 2000). Ambrose and others have explained the benefits of low-interest loans for homes and small businesses, and education training opportunities that transformed our country. Numerous other individuals, however, pointed out that the benefits were not equal for all groups of veterans. Beschloss (see Lehrer 2000) and Katznelson (2005) suggest that black Americans who received GI benefits could not use them in the same manner as their white counterparts. Many black veterans in the South could use their paid tuition credit only at segregated colleges that had limited career offerings. Further, access to information about veterans' benefits was limited in different parts of the country. It has been reported that job-finding assistance counselors were sparse in the South (Picker 2002). Even when they were available, the work for which many veterans were trained was not available to black veterans who lived in the segregated South.

Although some might think that these problems were confined to the South, black GIs who received low-interest housing loans were not welcomed in many middle-class communities throughout the country. The famous Levittown community in New York, which was built for the returning veterans of the Second World War and paid for by government-backed low-interest loans, was a segregated community. Beschloss (see Lehrer 2000) emphasized that in Levittown "You couldn't buy a house if you were black." The GI Bill inadvertently increased racial and economic inequities due to segregation and other government policies. It was not until the 1950s and 1960s that civil rights legislation and Supreme Court decisions provided some relief to black Americans.

By this time, white GIs had already had at least a 15-year advantage in building economic privilege. This translated to providing their families with new schools, recreational facilities, and homeownership. With the end of the Second World War, there was a confluence of forces that transformed American cities. The Federal Housing Administration (FHA) redlined urban areas or placed restrictions on property deeds in suburban communities to prevent minority ownership (Zubrinsky 1996) (see also chapter 3). Government spending on the interstate highway system provided a quick avenue to the suburbs (Caro 1974; Weingroff 2004). In the suburbs, developers built affordable housing, which could be purchased with low interest loans. With the development of affordable housing in the suburbs, the members of the new emerging middle class of the 1950s and 1960s were leaving urban areas. The void created by the migration of mostly white Americans to the suburbs was quickly filled by Latinos and other immigrants who joined black Americans looking for jobs in the manufacturing industries. This caused a drain on the economic base of many large cities because urban areas were losing their balance between low- and middle-class taxpayers. At the same time, the manufacturing industries that attracted semiskilled workers were beginning to relocate to the Sunbelt, thus leaving large pockets of unemployment which further degraded the urban landscape. Some of the newly settled urban neighborhoods, known as ghettos, barrios, or ethnic enclaves with high concentrations of homogeneous ethnic groups, shared a common characteristic of being left far from economic centers with few resources to counter the rise of homelessness and poverty (Evans 1994).

As the new middle class was moving into single-family homes, the urban renewal planners were placing low-income residents in towering complexes which resembled megawarehouses. The new housing plans, often referred to as "the projects," restricted one's daily interaction at street level. The neighborhood could no longer be observed and monitored from one's window. This was a form of what is referred to as spatial discrimination on a vertical scale. The

Chapter 8

suburbanites were building communities while the fabric of the urban neighborhoods was being decimated (Caro 1974; Jacobs 1992). In response to his critics, Robert Moses, who was labeled by biographer and Pulitzer Prize winner Robert Caro as a genius and influential seminal thinker, said, "I raise my stein to the builder who can remove ghettos without removing people as I hail the chef who can make omelets without breaking eggs" (Goldberger 1981, 3). Although the grand scale projects of the Moses years appear to have been replaced with a more subtle approach, economic segregation continues. Davis (1990) analyzed urban architecture, including the redevelopment of Bunker Hill in Los Angeles, and suggested that it benefits the wealthy and limits access of the poor. Traveling throughout California, it is evident that affluent areas are built almost as fortresses, separated from other communities by gates and cement-like walls. Davis also discussed Hunters Point in San Francisco that has required residents to have codes to enter the community. Taken a step further, communities have been restricting access to public parks and facilities with the issuance of leisure passes that required proof of residency to use the facility. As an example, communities such as San Marino, California, have kept its "public" parks closed on weekends to limit access to Latino and Asian Americans in neighboring communities (Davis 1990).

Davis's conclusions, still valid today, demonstrate that communities are contextualized by socioeconomic status, level of education, race, and ethnicity. The chapters in the present text corroborate Davis's findings by suggesting that more than anything else, socioeconomic status (SES) may predict additional characteristics of a particular neighborhood. Orfield, Bachmeier, James, and Eitle (1997) reported that SES not only categorizes a neighborhood economically, but also by race, ethnic background, and available opportunity.

Family and Communities Matter

All human factors have limits. It appears, however, to be politically incorrect to recognize the finite ability of schooling. The belief that schools alone can ameliorate the inequities faced by poor and excluded class students is entrenched in the American psyche. Some policymakers, politicians, and educators are quick to use the mantra "all people are created equal." True as it may be, it ends quickly at birth because it fails to realize that all people are not born into equal circumstances. The idea that education differences can be eradicated if students, teachers, parents, and administrators worked harder ignores the importance of out-of-school influences. It also ignores much of the research which suggests that differences between poor and affluent students increase the longer students remain in school (Johnson, Johnson, Farenga, and Ness 2005; Orfield et al. 1997; Rothstein 2004).

Over the last few decades, new methods were designed and thought to be the penicillin ready to revolutionize the field of education. Many school environments, however, appear to be resistant to change. New methods are introduced, teachers are trained, students are taught, and the test results for a large portion of the population remain stagnant. Why does the new penicillin constantly fail such a large group of students? The problem with most educational reform is that it forgets that students spend the majority of their time outside of school (Berliner 2005; Evans 2005).

Decades ago, James Coleman (1969) suggested that a school's influence on a student was marginal. His research highlighted the importance of parents and communities over schools. In support, Jencks and his colleagues reexamined the work of Coleman and corroborated his findings. The effect of the school depends on "the characteristics of the entering children. Everything else—the school budget, its policies, the characteristics of the teachers—is either secondary or completely irrelevant" (Jencks 1972, 255–256). To some, Coleman and Jencks were saying that if students entered school ahead they will leave ahead, and if they enter school behind, they will remain behind. In short, what was being done in school had little relationship to the success of students. The recognition and importance of environmental influences outside of the classroom had credible evidence to correlate experience and achievement.

Coleman and Jencks's ideas were viewed by some educators, researchers, and policymakers as heresy. The works of the two researchers were seen as a direct affront to the critics' beliefs and efforts (Evans 2005). The conclusions of Coleman and Jencks's research cast suspicion on a key component of Lyndon B. Johnson's Great Society program. At its heart was the conviction that educational reforms could create a new and better society ending poverty, improving healthcare, eliminating segregation, and increasing school aid (Hacsi 2002; Wolfensberger 2005). The idea that life's situations could not be improved simply by one's hard work at school was resisted (Evans 2005). After all, schooling and an education were considered the ticket out—the equalizer among people—the way to reach the middle class. Further, if schools could not eliminate the inequalities, a restructuring of public policy—corrective justice—would be needed. The failure of lawmakers to recognize the implications of the Coleman report—or to act on them—perpetuated the factors that increased inequities in education. If corrective justice had been undertaken 40 years ago, we might not have the education inequities described in this book.

The Playing Field from Birth to Preschool

When do we notice the differences? The differences among students are most prominent when students start school and appear again every September.

Research suggests that achievement differences appear well before kindergarten (Barton 2003; Lee and Burkam 2002). The differences in out-of-school related activities appear to widen the achievement gap and this gap further widens as students pass through the grades. The level of one's socio-economic status has been linked with children's readiness to begin school. On average, children from low-income households are one year behind middle-income students when they begin school (Lee and Burkam 2002).

We have argued that high-stakes testing must be discontinued because children from affluent families have an overwhelming advantage over children from financially impoverished households. That is, until we level the playing field between rich and poor, the current accountability movement in education that depends on high-stakes testing will only further widen the gap. We acknowledge, however, that from a cognitive standpoint, young children's informal activities during preschool free play time, show few significant differences in cognitive ability among children from low-income, middle-income, and upper-income backgrounds (Ginsburg, Pappas, and Seo 2001; Ness 2001). Four- and five-year-old children's problem solving abilities in the areas of informal mathematical tasks—such as determining the number of blocks needed to construct a foundation to a block house or avoiding obstacles when constructing various block structures—are evident regardless of social class (Ness 2001; Ness and Farenga 2007). These studies, however, included participants from low-income households who were fortunate to have had the opportunity to attend preschool programs, the expenses of which were subsidized by city and state funds as indicated by the Agency for Child Development Services (Ness 2001).

Research in cognitive and neuropsychology has demonstrated that the human nervous system is prewired in such a way that allows all human neonates and young children to respond to conditions in the environment on a generally equal footing. In other words, assuming that fetal development is on a successful course, these children of one, two, three, and possibly four years of age, regardless of race, ethnicity, gender, or social class, are on par from both a cognitive and neurological standpoint (Gleitman 1992; Gopnik, Meltzoff, and Kuhl 1999; Hertzman 2002). Social class difference, however, does have adverse effects on children who are raised in poverty. After infancy, the individual's cognitive and intellectual development is highly dependent on the kinds of life experiences to which that individual is exposed (Hertzman 2002; Hertzman and Wiens 1996). The prewired system is not hard-wired in the sense that the brain components and cognitive behavior remain static throughout the lifespan; on the contrary, the prewired brain is structured and constantly restructured in a flexible and dynamic manner, and brain and cognitive development are thus dependent on diverse life experiences. If the environment in which one lives does not sustain perceptual and behavioral tendencies to which the brain and nervous system are predisposed, the individual's opportunity for expression and refinement tends to become weaker (Gleitman 1992; Hertzman 2002; Nowakowski and Hayes 2002).

In terms of educational consequences, children who are either born or raised in impoverished conditions rarely have left their neighborhoods, more than likely have not attended a camp, and have not been to a museum, zoo, or aquarium. In contrast, other children as young as two or three years of age will hear about types of plants and animals when going on nature walks, for example, or learn about the different types of sea life when visiting an aquarium.

Hertzman (2002, 4) sums up the effects of childhood poverty in relationship to cognitive development: "Stimulation, support and nurturing play a role in brain development analogous to air quality in lung development. Spending one's early years in a relatively unstimulating, emotionally and physically unsupportive environment will limit the growth of the developing brain and lead to cognitive, social and behavioural delays that, in turn, will affect subsequent life chances."

Hertzman explains the disparate environmental conditions between children of rich and poor families in the Vancouver, British Columbia metropolitan area:

> In the affluent neighbourhoods on the west side of town, our study showed that approximately 3.5 percent of babies were born small for gestational age in 1996. In working class neighbourhoods, this figure rose above 10 percent, and rose again to over 18 percent in the impoverished downtown east side. Thus, a five-fold gradient for subsequent developmental risk was evident across the socioeconomic spectrum by the time of birth (4). (See also Hertzman, Kohen, McLean, Evans, and Dunn 2000)

Hertzman's findings show a direct relationship between living in poverty and giving birth to small or low birth weight infants. Children born into poverty as pre-term or full-term infants may lack stimulating and supportive environments in their everyday social settings. This lack of environmental stimulation often adversely affects children in poverty and their possibilities for success in school.

We cannot separate the equally important factors of 1) the prewired central nervous system—the experience-expectant explanation and 2) diverse life experiences after birth—the experience-dependent explanation (Bateson 1979; Greenough, Black, and Wallace 2002). The experience-expectant explanation proposes the existence of critical periods in which naturally occurring environmental stimuli are paired with the appropriate maturational readiness of the individual. These naturally occurring environmental experiences supply the required stimuli for the development of sensory organs and the brain. It is paramount, however, to time the experience with the readiness period. Brain formation is based on specific sensitive periods in which sensory system deprivation will adversely affect cognitive development (Feng and Rogowski 1980; Movshon and Van Sluyters 1981). That is, there are definitive periods in which natural environmental experiences must occur for the cognitive development and future functioning of the sensory organs.

The experience-dependent explanation involves the storage of environmental information that is experienced by the individual. The individual must be ready to act upon the stimuli and integrate them through the formation of new synaptic connections that form in response to the stimuli in the environment. The quality of the environmental stimuli may be the critical component of early enrichment in child development. Research suggests that there are critical periods in child development where deprivation will have lasting effects (Gopnik et al. 1999; Hertzman 2002). For example, Johnson and Johnson (2005) explain that humans have a critical period, a "window of opportunity," for initial language learning that begins to close between ages six and twelve: "Children who have been isolated from language input during those critical years have rarely developed language facility beyond that of a preschool child" (696).

The literature in cognitive science provides more detailed explanations of the negative impact of deprivation, but it does not provide specific formulae for the levels of enrichment that foster increased cognitive development (Gopnik et al. 1999). An important aspect of informal learning experiences may therefore be related to the experience-dependent explanation for the storage of information that is specific to the individual. That is, the more diverse the life experiences, the more positive the impact on solving problems. The less diverse the life experiences, the more negative the impact on future learning.

The Importance of Out-of-School Experiences

We have argued that stimulating environments are not only helpful but critical in the overall cognitive and intellectual development of the human being, and we have noted the disparities in experiences and stimulating environments during early childhood when comparing affluent children with those in poverty. This problem only gets worse when children are old enough to attend compulsory schooling (Johnson et al. 2005; Entwistle and Alexander 1992; Rothstein 2004). In general, all children, whether rich or poor, are expected to attend school by five or six years of age and must remain in school for at least 10 or 11 additional years. We have discussed the gross inequities between rich and poor children with regard to what is happening within the school environment, particularly the frenetic educational and political climate of high-stakes assessment.

What about outside of the school context? What life experiences do school-aged children of middle- or upper-income families have and how do these experiences compare with those of children of low-income families? In addition, how do these life experiences play a role in subsequent high-stakes testing conditions in formal academic environments? The short answer is that the potential life experiences of middle- and upper-income children are at best exhilarating and at worst promising, while those of low-income children as well as children of the excluded class are at best unstable and at worst, generally dismal or even harmful. Drawing from a variety of disciplines, including sociology (Epstein and Sanders 2000), developmental psychology (Piaget 1952; Vygotsky 1978), science education (Farenga 1995; Farenga and Joyce 1997; Marjoribanks 1991; Midwinter 1975), and mathematics education (Ness 2001; Saxe, Guberman, and Gearhart 1987), the importance of informal experience in transferring culturally vital information cannot be underestimated (Brown, Collins, and Duguid 1989).

The academic achievement gap appears to grow over the summer (Allington and McGill-Franzen 2003). *Summer loss,* a term described by Gerald Bracey (2002), needs earnest consideration. Low-income students seem to regress over the summer period, but students from the middle class and upper middle class continue to advance. Entwistle and Alexander (1992) suggested that when students from low-income families enter middle school, the achievement gap may escalate to more than two years. What is the effect of out-of-school learning related experiences? A review of out-of-school programs for students at risk shows promise for these children (Lauer, Akiba, Wilkerson, Apthrop, Snow, and Martin-Glenn 2006). Whether programs are scheduled after the school day or during the summer makes little difference; most programs provide the students with some academic benefit. In general, programs must be at least 45 hours in duration, well-conceived, and staffed with trained teachers. The most effective programs have flexible groups and include one-on-one tutoring. De Kanter (2001) claims that only 6 million of the 54 million children in the United States participate in after-school programs. The majority of these children are from middle-class and upper-income backgrounds; 89 percent of the potentially eligible students are not benefiting from out-of-school programs.

Life Experience at Camp

Camps and the camping industry are a $20 billion a year business (Sabin 2006). According to the National Camp Association, approximately 6.5 million children attend camp each year (Gormly 2005). The part-time camps staffed by teachers and others during the summer months have gone the way of the dodo bird and passenger pigeon. Today's camps are full-time businesses that are run like educational agencies. Camps have their own accrediting body, the American Camp Association (ACA 2006a), which has over 6,700 members and accredits more than 2,300 camps. Like all accrediting bodies, the ACA has specific requirements for personnel, camper/staff ratios, safety, work experience, and programs. The ACA lists over 300 standards for health, safety, and program quality that are to be met to obtain accreditation (ACA 2006b). For example, the ACA sets minimum requirements for directors of camps that include a baccalaureate degree, camp administration experience, and in-service training (Frost 2006). The ACA specifies additional requirements for nurses and other personnel.

Many camps have become extensions of the school year for a privileged group of students. The modern-day camps have become enrichment hubs that can fulfill most students' desires. Camp programs are as diverse as Michigan's Interlochen Arts Camp and the U.S. Space Camp in Huntsville, Alabama (Frost 2006). Some camps specialize in an interest (e.g., robotics), a career (e.g., aviation/pilots), or a talent (e.g., gymnastics). Some camps are residential and others are day camps with no overnight facilities. The lists of camps and descriptions provided by Frost (2006) and Gormly (2005) are lengthy. We include a sample list in table 8.1. Children whose parents have the money are given opportunities to engage in the fine arts, the sciences and technology, athletics, the culinary arts, mechanics, the performing arts, leadership training, and more.

TABLE 8.1.
Sample List of Camp Types

Camps*	General Description
Science/Mathematics/ Technology-related camps	
U.S. Space Camp, Space Academy and Advanced Space Camp	Astronaut training and simulations aboard the space shuttle, orbiter, and space station. Age-specific programs (9–11 Space Camp, 12–14 Space Academy, 15–18 Advanced Space Camp).
Carnegie Science Center	Summer science programs for children ages four through 13.
Camp Invention	Enhances science, mathematics, history, and the arts as well as recreation.
Zoo camp (hosted by numerous zoos throughout the country)	Animal husbandry/Animal science/Behavioral training techniques. Specialty programs (e.g., insect investigation, animals with poisons and venom, primates) are age specific and generally range from pre-K to 12th grade.
Sea camp	Generally includes the study of oceanography, biology, ecology, and physiology. Can also focus on career opportunities in these fields.
Sports-related camps	
Tennis camp	Physical training, fundamentals of the sport from proper footwork and grips to stroke production and movement. Programs are generally divided by levels: beginner, intermediate, and advanced.

TABLE 8.1.
(continued)

Camps	General Description
Basketball camp	Builds skills in basketball (e.g., footwork, ball handling, teamwork), and learning the fine points of the sport.
Golf camp	Mind and mechanics of the game. Develops golf swing fundamentals, concentration skills, rules and etiquette.
Gymnastics camp	Builds skills in gymnastics, learning the fine points of the sport (i.e., emphasis placed on fundamentals, body positions, and skill acquisition).
Swimming and diving camp	Builds skills in swimming (novice and competitive swimmers) and diving (springboard and platform divers), and learning the fine points of the sports.
Equestrian camp	Learning the fine aspects of horsemanship safety, ground handling, grooming, and the use and care of equipment.
Baseball camp	Builds skills in baseball (i.e., hitting, throwing, fielding, and speed/agility), and learning the fine points of the sport.
Arts-related camps	
Camp Broadway	Camp Broadway produces theater programs and workshops. Programs are based in New York City, but many are also presented in locations throughout the United States. Children from 6 to 17 years of age.
Aspen Music Festival and School (Aspen, Colorado)	Residential musical training-ground for the next generation of musicians.
Tanglewood Music Festival	Residential music school—the oldest in the United States (Lenox, Massachusetts).
Language camp	Language camps are based throughout the United States and Canada and are both day and residential.
Clown Camp	Week-long clown training program—the oldest in existence—headquartered at the University of Wisconsin at LaCrosse.
Writing camp	Numerous camps dedicated to the art of writing. Some include Inner Spark (Valencia, California) and Johns Hopkins Summer Writing Program (Baltimore, MD).
Outdoor-related camps	
Archaeology/Paleontology	Camps that provide students with the opportunity to learn excavation, identifying fossils, and learning about culture and past life.
Orienteering/Survival	Campers learn to identify one location using the natural surrounding, reading maps and star charts, using a compass, and being able to survive in the wilderness.
Naturalist Training camp	Campers engage in the study of the ecological processes in a variety of field environments.
Camps at sea	These take place at sea. Foci may vary: marine science, nautical training, travel and adventure.

*There are approximately 10,000 children's summer camps in the United States, and 60 percent are residential camps (Gormly 2005).

As a former camp director and educational program planner for sleepover camps, one of the authors of this text affirms that there are a number of skills and attitudes that are fostered at camp beyond content knowledge. Students learn independence, responsibility, self-reliance, the art of making friends, and engagement in creative activities—all important life-enhancing lessons. The ACA's definition of "camping" reinforces the skills and attitudes that are developed by a successful camp's programs. ACA defines camping as "a sustained experience that provides a creative, recreational, and educational opportunity in group living in the outdoors. It utilizes trained leadership and the resources of the natural surroundings to contribute to each camper's mental, physical, social, and spiritual growth" (ACA 2006a, 1). Three of the four ACA goals that are mentioned in the definition of camping plainly parallel the desired outcomes of any educational program (i.e., mental, physical, and social growth).

Table 8.2 is a sample of a day camp schedule for an upper camp (grades four through six). In upper camp, campers are divided not only by age, but also by gender. Day camp programs are generally Monday through Friday

TABLE 8.2.
A Generic Day Camp Schedule

Group Name: Wild Cats
Counselor's Name: Joe W.
Counselor in Training: Timmy   Number of Campers: 10

Time	Activity	Comments
8:45–9:00	Administrative duties	Pledge, attendance, lunch slips
9:00–10:00	Swimming (lessons)	If rain, racquetball, paddleball, or indoor tennis
10:00–11:00	Boating (sailing, rowing, or power)	If rain, gymnasium (basketball, volleyball, rope climbing)
11:00–12:00	Art, drama, music	Inform specialist of any change in schedule if you intend to substitute activity (e.g., fishing, remain at boat house)
12:00–12:45	Lunch (in Outdoor Area A, tables 17 through 19)	If rain, lower level cafeteria
12:45–1:00	Downtime	Return to bunker (the Den)
1:00–2:00	Science center	Ecology, computer room, or aviation center
2:00–3:00	Team sports activity (e.g., baseball, soccer, field hockey)	Large athletic field
3:00–4:00	Pool (free swim)	If rain, return to the Den. Knock hockey, ping pong, or any other indoor board game
4:00–4:15	Snack (pick up in Kitchen Area B, in Outdoor Area A, tables 17 through 19)	If rain, bring snack back to the Den

TABLE 8.2.
(continued)

Group Name: Wild Cats
Counselor's Name: Joe W.
Counselor in Training: Timmy   *Number of Campers: 10*

Time	Activity	Comments
4:15–4:30	Review the day's activities, prepare for the next day, and bring campers to loading area.	Be sure campers have all notices and get required medications and any other items to bring home.
4:30	Load buses	Take attendance on the bus, be sure all campers are accounted for, and drive safely.

Please check for daily special events (e.g., go carts, Color War activities, and carnival).

from 8:00 A.M. to 6:00 P.M. Campers are bused to the location or are dropped off by parents. Day camp usually begins with a formation and a meeting with one's group. The "Pledge of Allegiance" is recited, roll call is taken, lunch slips are sent to the kitchen, medicines are handed to the nurse, and counselors and campers are off to the first of the day's activities. Activities for the groups in the upper camp are usually scheduled into 60-minute blocks of time.

Table 8.3 is a sample of a residential camp schedule for grades five and six. Residential camps are generally coeducational, but for specific activities, the groups may be divided by gender. Dining, free time, and waterfront activities, however, may provide time for interaction between boys and girls. Residential camp programs range from one to nine weeks in duration, and counselors are expected to monitor campers around the clock. The campers' parents either make their own arrangements for transportation to the camp or take advantage of a transportation option that may be offered by the camp administration. The sample schedule is a typical day in a residential camp. The day begins at 7:00 in the morning for "rise and shine" and preparation for the first day's activity. Roll call is taken, and campers requiring medicines go to the nurse. Activities for the groups in the residential camp are usually scheduled into 60- to 105-minute blocks of time.

The campers' schedules in tables 8.2 and 8.3 show that many of the camp activities are school-related. One might consider camp as a residential, hands-on school. Campers are given the opportunity to learn by doing in a non-threatening environment. The children are learning while they are enjoying themselves. In addition, there are more opportunities at camp for children to be physically active and avoid sedentary behaviors. A middle school science teacher from an affluent district in New York told us:

Having not gone to a residential camp myself, I am amazed how my students cannot wait for school to end to attend camp. The lessons and stories that some

TABLE 8.3.
A Generic Residential Camp Schedule

Group Name: Timberland
Counselor's Name: Lisa M.
Counselor's Name: Mike T.   Number of Campers: 15

Time	Activity	Comments
7:00	Rise and shine	Get ready for early morning activity that was selected on the previous evening.
7:15	Early morning activity	Optional, based on camper interest.*
8:00	Kitchen patrol	Report to dining hall for breakfast duty.
8:10	Line up for breakfast	Campers form single lines by group.
8:15	Breakfast	Remind campers to take only what they can eat.
9:00	Return to dorms	Make beds, clean dorm, get ready for the remainder of the morning's activities.
9:30	First scheduled morning activity	Select from one of the activities listed below.*
10:45	Second scheduled morning activity	Select from one of the activities listed below that was not selected for the first activity.*
12:00 (noon)	Kitchen patrol to dining hall	Setup for lunch.
12:10	Line up for lunch	Campers form single lines by group.
12:15	Lunch	Remind campers to take only what they can eat.
1:15	Leave dining hall to return to bunks and prepare for the afternoon	Downtime. Send any camper who needs medication to the nurse. Remaining campers may read, go to the nature center, walk by the lake, sit on the lawn by the bunk house.
2:00	First scheduled afternoon activity	Select from one of the activities listed below that was not selected for the first or second activity.**
3:00	Second scheduled afternoon activity	Select from one of the activities listed below that was not selected for the first, second, or third activity.**
4:00	Free time activity	Campers may swim, canoe, go fishing, go to the sports center, craft center, or nature center.

TABLE 8.3.
(continued)

Group Name: Timberland
Counselor's Name: Lisa M.
Counselor's Name: Mike T.   Number of Campers: 15

Time	Activity	Comments
5:45	Kitchen patrol to dining hall	Setup for dinner.
5:55	Line up for dinner	Campers form single lines by group.
6:00	Dinner	Remind campers to take only what they can eat.
7:00	Send any campers who need medication to the nurse; return with the other campers to dorms	Downtime, prepare for evening program; collect any medication from campers that need to be given later in the evening.
7:15	Evening program	Special Activity/Presentation (e.g., the World of Mammals, the Reptile Man, Wildlife Rehabilitators with Birds of Prey).
8:15	Campfire/Sing-along	Make sure campers have used their insect repellant. If rain, return to the all-purpose building.
9:15	Night walk and back to dorms	Weather permitting, constellation sighting.
10:00	Lights out	Check that all campers are in their bunks ready to go to sleep.

* Sample of morning activities: Pond ecology, wildlife studies, field ecology, forest ecology, stream ecology.
** Sample of afternoon activities: Mountain trail hiking, geology, ornithology, pond studies, orienteering (maps and compasses).

of my students share about camp and their travel experiences are enlightening. The students are often able to relate many of the abstract topics in the science curriculum to the direct experiences they have had during the summer. When studying rock formations that are present in the Grand Canyon, it's surprising the number of students who are able to provide first-hand knowledge of what the rocks look like, how they're positioned, and the fossil formations that are present. . . . Unfortunately, it is easy to detect the differences between the students who are actively engaged in summertime programs and those who have fewer summer opportunities and spend their time hanging out, watching television, playing videogames, playing CDs, surfing the Internet without purpose, and walking the malls.

The advantages of camps are not limited to the summer months; camps are year-round businesses. There are camps that operate during the winter months and international camps with a variety of climates that are available to students during winter recess and long holiday vacations. It is not uncommon for children of affluent backgrounds to return to school after winter recess and say that they have returned from cross-country skiing or figure skating camp in the mountains of Vermont, Utah, Colorado, or even overseas in Switzerland.

In most cases, the educational experiences between children of the excluded class and affluent students are quantitatively and qualitatively unequal. There is little, if anything, for students who do not participate in summer programs or travel to share with the class—except to tell about the test-prep summer school they had to attend because of low scores on the spring high-stakes test. Their formal schooling and informal learning opportunities are effectively put on hold until September. The students who are engaged in a program for most of the summer appear to be primed for school schedules and activities. These students have the opportunity to transfer knowledge between the formal content taught in school and the practical applications found in the field (i.e., camp, travel). For these students, the major problem is reacclimating to the culture of school. Students who are not engaged in summer programs also need to grapple with the return to school culture, and at the same time, prepare for formal learning experiences. Students, many of whom are from impoverished communities, and who come from backgrounds or environments where they are not engaged in activities that are transferable to skills and content taught in school, are at a disadvantage.

The cost of residential camps (i.e., sleep-away camps) will vary depending on the duration of the stay, the camp's reputation, areas of specialty, size, and location. "One-week sessions, where available, range from $400 to $2,000. Two-week sessions will range in cost from $800 to $4,000. Four-week sessions will cost from $1,500 to $6,000. Full season camps, lasting from seven to nine weeks, will range from $3,000 to $9,000" (National Camping Association 2006). It is no wonder, then, why millions of American children are unable to attend summer camp. Gormly (2005) reports that some parents consider camps a necessity despite the increasing camp costs. Some families may find day camps to be moderately priced daycare. The expense may seem reasonable for childcare eight hours per day and five days per week. For the excluded class, however, camp of any sort is not in the picture.

It can be said that we are the sum total of the decisions and experiences that we have made and have had throughout our lives. It is clear that people exist in socioeconomic political contexts that shape their lives and worldview. The effects of mediated learning experiences on an individual cannot be underestimated. Students from middle-class and upper-middle class families are in homes which often can provide educational materials such as books and computers, and they are involved in more out-of-school experiences. Less fortunate students often are left to fend for themselves. The deck is stacked against those who are poor, because they must take the same high-stakes tests as those children who have it all.

Mary Budd Rowe (1978, 459), in reference to a Wordsworth poem, writes, "The environment of children is mostly people and nature. Out of their interactions with these two, children one day become men and women. What will they be like? Wordsworth said, 'The Child is father to the Man.' How then shall we treat these fathers and mothers of future men and women? What is our dream for them?" For too many of America's children, the treatment is shameful and the dream already is shattered.

References

Allington, R., and A. McGill-Franzen. 2003. The impact of summer setback on the reading achievement gap. *Phi Delta Kappan* 85 (September): 68–75.

American Camp Association (ACA). 2006a. What does accreditation mean? www .acacamps.org/accreditation/whatdoes.php (accessed July 13, 2006).

———. 2006b. Standards at a glance. www.acacamps.org/accreditation/stdsglance.php (accessed July 13, 2006).

American Federation of Teachers (AFT). 2006. Funding gap persists between rich and poor school districts. *American Teacher* 90 (7): 6.

Barton, P. E. 2003. *The achievement gap: Baselines for tracking progress.* Princeton, NJ: Educational Testing Service Policy Information.

Bateson, P. P. G. 1979. How do sensitive periods arise and what are they for? *Animal Behavior* 27:470–486.

Berliner, D. C. 2005. Our impoverished view of educational reform. *Teachers College Record* 108 (6): 949–995.

Bracey, G. W. 2002. Summer loss: The phenomenon no one wants to deal with. *Phi Delta Kappan* 84 (September): 12–13.

Brown, J. S., A. Collins, and P. Duguid. 1989. Situated cognition and the culture of learning. *Educational Researcher* 18 (1): 32–42.

Caro, R. 1974. *The power broker: Robert Moses and the fall of New York.* New York: Knopf.

Coleman, J. 1969. *Equality of educational opportunity.* Washington, DC: U.S. Government Printing Office.

———. 1988. Social capital in the creation of human capital. *American Journal of Sociology* 94:95–120.

Davis, M. 1990. *City of quartz.* New York: Vintage Books.

De Kanter, A. 2001. After-school programs for adolescents. *NASSP Bulletin* 85 (626): 12–21.

Entwistle, D. R., and K. L. Alexander. 1992. Summer setback: Race, poverty, school composition, and mathematics achievement in the first two years of school. *American Sociological Review* 57:72–84.

Epstein, J. L., and M. G. Sanders. 2000. Connecting home, school, and community: New directions for social research. In *Handbook of the sociology of education,* ed. M. T. Hallinan, 285–306. New York: Kluwer Academic/Plenum Publishers.

Evans, K. 1994. Urban youth gangs: The interplay of structural forces. *Berkeley McNair Journal* 2 (summer). www-mcnair.berkeley.edu/94BerkeleyMcNairJournal/16_Evans.html (accessed July 1, 2006).

Evans, R. 2005. Reframing the achievement gap. *Phi Delta Kappan* 86 (April): 582–589.

Farenga, S. J. 1995. Out-of-school science-related experiences, science attitudes, and the selection of science mini-courses by high ability, upper elementary students. Ed.D. dissertation, Columbia University.

Farenga, S. J., and B. Joyce. 1997. What children bring to the classroom: Learning science from experience. *School Science and Mathematics* 97 (5): 248–252.

Feng, A. S., and B. A. Rogowski. 1980. Effects of monaural and binaural occlusion on the morphology of neurons in the medial superior olivary nucleus of the rat. *Brain Research* 189:530–534.

Frost, D. 2006. Finding the best camp for your child.www.gocamps.com/articparent.html (accessed July 9, 2006).

Ginsburg, H. P., S. Pappas, and K. H. Seo. 2001. Everyday mathematical knowledge: Asking young children what is developmentally appropriate. In *Psychological Perspectives on Early Childhood Education,* ed. S. L. Golbeck, 181–219. Mahwah, NJ: Lawrence Erlbaum Associates.

Gleitman, H. 1992. *Basic psychology.* 3rd ed. New York: Norton.

Goldberger, P. 1981. Robert Moses, master builder, is dead at 92. *New York Times,* July 30. www.nytimes.com/learning/general/onthisday/bday/1218.html (accessed July 13, 2006).

Gopnik, A., A. N. Meltzoff, and P. K. Kuhl. 1999. *The scientist in the crib: What early learning tells us about the mind.* New York: Harper Collins.

Gormly, K. B. 2005. Specialty programs expand the definition of "camp." *Pittsburgh Tribune-Review,* May 24. www.pittsburghlive.com/x/pittsburghtrib/s_337226.html (accessed July 13, 2006).

Greenough, W. T., J. E. Black, and C. S. Wallace. 2002. Experience and brain development. In *Brain development and cognition: A reader,* ed. M. H. Johnson, Y. Munakata, and R. O. Gilmore, 186–216. Malden, MA: Blackwell Publishing.

Hacsi, T. A. 2002. *Children as pawns: The politics of educational reform.* Cambridge, MA: Harvard University Press.

Hertzman, C. 2002. *Leave no child behind: Social exclusion and child development.* Toronto: Laidlaw Foundation.

Hertzman, C., D. Kohen, S. McLean, T. Evans, and J. Dunn. 2000. First report on the early development and community asset mapping project. Report submitted to the Vancouver-Richmond Health Department.

Hertzman, C., and M. Wiens. 1996. Child development and long-term outcomes: A population health perspective and summary of successful interventions. *Social Sciences and Medicine* 43:1083–1095.

Jacobs, J. 1992. *The death and life of great American cities.* New York: Vintage. (Originally published 1961.)

Jencks, C. 1972. *Inequality: A reassessment of the effect of family and schooling in America.* New York: Basic Books.

Johnson, D. D., and Johnson, B. 2005. Language development. In *Encyclopedia of education and human development, volume 3,* eds. S. J. Farenga and D. Ness, 688–717. Armonk, NY: M. E. Sharpe.

Johnson, D. D., B. Johnson, S. Farenga, and D. Ness. 2005. *Trivializing teacher education: The accreditation squeeze.* Lanham, MD: Rowman & Littlefield.

Katznelson, I. 2005. *When affirmative action was white: An untold history of racial inequality in twentieth-century America.* New York: Norton.

Lauer, P. A., M. Akiba, S. B. Wilkerson, H. S. Apthorp, D. Snow, and M. L. Martin-Glenn. 2006. Out-of-school-time programs: A meta-analysis of effects for at-risk students. *Review of Educational Research* 76 (2): 275–313.

Lee, V. E., and D. T. Burkam. 2002. *Inequality at the starting gate: Social background differences in achievement as children begin school.* Washington, DC: Economic Policy Institute.

Lehrer, J. 2000. Remembering the GI Bill. NewsHour with Jim Lehrer transcript, Public Broadcasting System. July 4. www.pbs.org/newshour/bb/military/july-dec00/gibill_7-4.html (accessed June 18, 2006).

Marjoribanks, K. 1991. Educational productivity and talent development. In *Families, schools, and students' educational outcomes,* eds. B. J. Fraser and H. J. Walberg, 75–91. New York: Pergamon Press.

Midwinter, E. 1975. Toward a solution of the EPA problem: The community school. In *Education and deprivation,* eds. J. Rushton and J. D. Turner, 159–183. Manchester: Manchester University Press.

Movshon, J. A., and R. C. Van Sluyters. 1981. Visual neuronal development. *Annual Review of Psychology* 32:477–522.

National Camping Association. 2006. How to choose a summer camp. National Camping Association. www.summercamp.org/guidance/pamphlet.html (accessed July 1, 2006).

Ness, D. 2001. The development of spatial thinking, emergent geometric concepts, and architectural principles in the everyday context. PhD diss., Columbia University.

Ness, D., and Farenga, S. 2007. *Knowledge under construction: The importance of play in developing children's spatial and geometric thinking.* Lanham, MD: Rowman & Littlefield.

Nowakowski, R. S., and N. L. Hayes. 2002. General principles in central nervous system (CNS) development. In *Brain development and cognition: A reader,* eds. M. H. Johnson, Y. Munakata, and R. O. Gilmore, 57–82. Malden, MA: Blackwell Publishing.

Orfield, G., M. D. Bachmeier, D. R. James, and T. Eitle. 1997. *Deepening segregation in American public schools.* Cambridge, MA: Harvard Project on School Desegregation.

Piaget, J. 1952. *The origins of intelligence in children.* New York: International Universities Press.

Picker, L. 2002. The G.I. Bill, World War II, and the education of black Americans. National Bureau of Economic Research. www.nber.org/digest/dec02/w9044.html (accessed June 18, 2006).

Rothstein, R. 2004. *Class and schools: Using social, economic, and educational reform to close the black-white achievement gap.* New York: Teachers College Columbia University and Washington, DC: Economic Policy Institute.

Rowe, M. B. 1978. *Teaching science as continuous inquiry.* New York: McGraw-Hill.

Sabin, J. 2006. Notes on camp: Executives quit the rat race to manage the sack race. *New York,* July 17, 12.

Saxe, G. B., S. R. Guberman, and M. Gearhart. 1987. Social processes in early number development. *Monographs of the Society for Research in Child Development* 52:2.

Vygotsky, L. 1978. *Mind in society.* Cambridge, MA: Harvard University Press.

Weingroff, R. F. 2004. The genie in the bottle: The interstate system and urban problems, 1939–1957. U.S. Department of Transportation: Federal Highway Administration. www.fhwa.dot.gov/infrastruture/rw00c.htm (accessed July 2, 2006).

Winter, G. 2004. Financial gap is widening for rich and poor schools. *New York Times,* October 6, A19.

Wolfensberger, D. 2005. Congress and education policy: ESEA at 40. Woodrow Wilson International Center for Scholars. March 15. www.wilsoncenter.org/events/docs/education-intro.pdf (accessed July 11, 2006).

Zubrinsky, C. L. 1996. "I have always wanted to have a neighbor, just like you . . .": Race and residential segregation in the city of Los Angeles. PhD diss., University of California, Los Angeles. Ann Arbor, MI: UMI Dissertation Services.

Afterword

PUBLIC SCHOOL, FOR MANY AMERICAN CHILDREN, has been transformed by politicians and political appointees. Instead of recognizing the individual differences among children and youth, their cultural backgrounds, interests, needs, and rates of learning, all students in a grade now are expected to perform at a designated level of competence on standardized tests. The public school has been transformed from an institution dedicated to fostering children's individuality, creativity, understanding, and eagerness to learn into an institution where the primary focus is preparing for a test through narrowly focused drills, rehearsals, and repetition. Public schools were places where innovative, well-prepared teachers could design instruction geared to their students' abilities and needs; now they are places where state- or federally mandated "standards" must be followed precisely in every class because of the ultimate high-stakes tests.

The public school has been changed from an institution where children and youth were engaged in art, music, and drama; where they discussed and debated issues large and small; where they studied the social sciences and the hard sciences; to an institution where much of their time is directed to reading and math exercises as defined by standards and high-stakes tests. Public schools were viewed as sheltered environments where children could feel safe and enjoy their varied learning experiences. Now, for many American children, public school is a place of stress and tension, of tears and illness brought on by high-stakes testing repression enacted and enforced by elected state and federal officials and their minions in appointed positions of authority. In less than a decade, the pleasures of learning and teaching have been squeezed out of many public schools by poorly conceived notions of school improvement as determined by individuals far removed from any real, recent classroom experience as either a learner or a teacher.

Public schools were places where budget monies were allocated for library books and resources, field trips, and hands-on learning experiences. They now are places where the budget is spent on test-preparation worksheets, workbooks, software, consultants, for-profit tutoring businesses, and the accountability fiefdoms that have developed at all levels to perpetuate this new status quo.

In every state in the nation there are public schools that have it all and public schools that have little. Schools in communities with a strong tax base enjoy new or remodeled and refurbished school buildings with well-stocked libraries, computer and science labs, swimming pools, and a well-rounded curriculum. Schools in communities with a weak tax base often are housed in worn-out, vermin-infested buildings with outdated equipment and inadequate resources and a largely test-prep curriculum. Students who attend the former schools typically come from middle class and affluent families. Students in the latter schools come from families with limited incomes and the miseries of poverty. In each state, students from both types of schools take the same high-stakes tests. Schools that do well are lauded and applauded. Schools that do poorly are shamed and punished.

We have seen that the medical and dental problems of poor and minority children are far greater than those of affluent children. Poor children are more likely to witness or experience violence at home, in school, or in the community. They are more likely to attend underfunded schools, and they rarely enjoy the out-of-school enrichment experiences that middle- and upper-income children do. Children of the excluded class are likely to live in substandard housing and many of them come to school hungry. The deck is stacked against them on high-stakes tests.

The use of tests to pressure teachers and students to work harder is a senseless and mean-spirited policy. The perpetrators of these mandates—the Business Roundtable, politicians, and policymakers—should know that instead of enhancing education, high-stakes tests are restricting and diminishing genuine teaching and learning. Michael Winerip was an education columnist for *The New York Times* for four years. In his final column (July 12, 2006), he explained that it was teachers who took him to "the heart of education," who showed him what schooling could be. It wasn't chancellors, commissioners, or secretaries of education. In defense of teachers at a time when they seem to be easy targets for all of society's failings, Winerip writes:

> I'm not a fan of No Child Left Behind, the 2002 federal law aimed at raising education quality. Instead of helping teachers, for me it's a law created by politi-

cians who distrust teachers. Because teachers' judgment and standards are supposedly not reliable, the law substitutes a battery of tests that are supposed to tell the real truth about children's academic progress. The question is: How successful can an education law be that makes teachers the enemy?

A final concern with the federal law is that it is so driven by state testing that there's too much time devoted to test prep, too much time spent drilling facts for survey courses, and not enough emphasis on finding something children will fall in love with for a lifetime—the Civil War, repairing engines, science research, playing the trumpet. (C13)

Our public school system can take one of three paths. The first path is the status quo. Public education can continue to be directed and shaped by noneducators through the use of standards, accountability, and high-stakes testing even though research has shown that half of the more than 800 high-stakes state tests don't even line up with the state standards (Keller 2006). In other words, teachers who teach to the state standards are doing their students a disservice when it comes to the high-stakes tests they must pass. With the status quo, teachers can continue to be seen as "the enemies" as Winerip put it, rather than held in esteem as are teachers in other countries (see the discussion of Finland in chapter 1). And the children who fail the tests, mostly the poor and minorities, can continue to be sorted, labeled, shamed, flunked, denied graduation several times over, or pushed to drop out of school.

The second path would alter substantially the life chances of poor and minority children, but it would take a national will and commitment and many years to achieve. That path is the establishment of corrective justice. The path could begin with a major increase in the minimum wage that has been stagnant for 10 years despite 25 percent salary increases for Congress during that period. Corrective justice would require the creation of jobs with adequate pay, the construction of low-cost housing, the establishment of a system of guaranteed medical care for all Americans, and a renewed war on poverty and homelessness. Corrective justice would require a redistribution of wealth made possible by the return of a strong, progressive income tax after years of tax cuts for the rich. Such an effort would require billions of dollars, but our politicians have been able to find billions of dollars to spend on an unpopular war. Corrective justice could, in time, eliminate the class differences that have stacked the deck against America's poor and minorities in the public schools. Will any U.S. president or Congress have the courage and determination to help our own citizens by making corrective justice the major national priority?

The third path also would require gumption by elected leaders. This path would discontinue all public school accountability systems as they now exist with their heavy reliance on high-stakes testing and punitive consequences. It would require the leadership of the president and Congress to repeal the No Child Left Behind Act. Next, state governors and legislators, mayors and school superintendents would need to muster the courage to buck big business to repeal all laws and mandates that undergird high-stakes testing. Then the test-driven curriculum and test-driven instruction could just stop.

Most of our readers will remember what public school was like when they were students—before all of the high-stakes testing began. They remember school as a time of exploration and learning. They can recite the names of some of their elementary school teachers. They remember taking art, music, and physical education and reminisce about special units and class projects. They remember having a recess in the morning and in the afternoon, something that now has been taken away in many public schools. They recall library books, field trips, heated discussions, and group activities. These things still are true in some schools today, but rarely are so in the schools that serve poor and minority children.

If high-stakes testing were discontinued and teachers regained some of their lost autonomy, their real teaching talents—their ability to individualize instruction—quickly would resurface, we predict. If high-stakes testing were discontinued, perhaps the bright, creative teachers who have left teaching because they saw children's hopes destroyed by high-stakes tests could be lured back into teaching. Maybe the numerous stressed-out children and youth could participate in a more intellectually productive curriculum. Perhaps all the billions of dollars that are being squandered on the testing and tutoring enterprises could be redirected to things that matter in public schools—children, teachers, experiences, and resources.

A small beam of hope appeared on the public school horizon as this book went to press. The hope came from the publication, *Tough Choices or Tough Times: The Report of the New Commission on the Skills of the American Workforce* (National Center on Education and the Economy 2007). The report describes problems in American education but argues, "The problem is not with our educators. It is with the system in which they work" (9). *Tough Choices* called for many of the suggestions articulated in the present volume:

- Schools serving students from low-income families and other categories of disadvantaged students would get substantially more money than schools with more advantaged student bodies (16–17).
- Disadvantaged students will . . . get the eyeglasses they need or the hearing aids or the therapy for dyslexia or any of the many other things that have prevented these children from learning as well as their wealthier peers. These schools will be able to afford the tutors they need, the counselors and mentors that are the birthright of richer children elsewhere (18).

- High-quality, universal early childhood education . . . [will be provided] to its three- and four-year-olds (17).
- A very high level of preparation in reading, writing, speaking, mathematics, science, literature, history, and the arts will be an indispensable foundation for everything that comes after (6).

Such breadth of curriculum would replace today's concentration on math and reading to the exclusion of most other subjects.

- Too often, our testing system rewards students who will be good at routine work, while not providing opportunities for students to display creative and innovative thinking and analysis (9).

This welcome return to a curriculum designed to allow creativity and innovation would replace the rigid, punitive, standardized testing and teaching described throughout this book.

- We would have teachers be employed by the state, not the local districts. . . . The state would . . . write performance contracts with schools of education, but also teachers' collaboratives, school districts, and others interested in training teachers (14).

Current teacher education policies such as the cumbersome, time-wasting, political teacher accreditation processes now in place would be eliminated.

Tough Choices or Tough Times is a condemnation of present education policies and a clarion call for real reform.

We close this volume with the words of Louella Swanson, a teacher in a Long Island elementary school that serves mostly black children of poverty. Louella said,

> We have a new superintendent at my school, and he said that our children are equal to all other children. They are just as smart and intelligent. They can learn; they can get fours [the highest score rating on New York tests].
>
> Our children are equal to other children. But the injustice, abuse, malnutrition, inconsistency, and lack of refuge steal their ability to achieve what most children can. In developing countries, we accept that children have difficult lives and only money and support can help them build to be something better. A child of a third-world ghetto isn't expected to receive a four to insure financial aid; the child is only expected to improve with assistance. The homes my students live in are like the third world. My teaching experience in India was more positive than in my district here on Long Island. Drug abuse, corruption, and unachievable goals have been placed upon my students and me. I teach special education, and

my students' future isn't rosy. They live very dangerous lives. They only have a few years until they are gobbled up by a gang or something else that wants to take them. I need to provide them with skills and I need to nourish their souls because they deserve it and because something in them could strengthen and could survive.

References

Keller, B. 2006. States' standards, tests are a mismatch, study finds. *Education Week,* July 26, 5, 20.

National Center on Education and the Economy. 2007. *Tough Choices or Tough Times: The Report of the New Commission on the Skills of the American Workforce: Executive Summary.* www.skillscommission.org.

Winerip, M. 2006. Teachers, and a law that distrusts them. *New York Times,* July 12, C13.

Index

About the Authors

Dale D. Johnson is a professor of literacy education at Dowling College, Long Island, New York. Dr. Johnson was a professor at the University of Wisconsin-Madison for twenty years and at colleges and universities in Iowa and Louisiana. He served as the dean of the College of Education and Human Development at the University of Louisiana at Monroe, spent several years as an elementary and middle school teacher, and was elected to the presidency of the International Reading Association. Dr. Johnson taught English as a second language in Katsina, Nigeria. His research centers on vocabulary development and comprehension. Dr. Johnson is the author of fifteen books; numerous scholarly articles; and instructional materials for children, adolescents, and adults. His most recent books are *Vocabulary in the Elementary and Middle School*; *High Stakes: Poverty, Testing, and Failure in American Schools*; and *Trivializing Teacher Education: The Accreditation Squeeze*. Dr. Johnson earned his Ph.D. at the University of Wisconsin-Madison.

Bonnie Johnson is professor of human development and learning at Dowling College, Long Island, New York. She has held professorial positions in Louisiana, Texas, and Iowa. Dr. Johnson has taught at all levels from preschool through graduate school. She was awarded the Distinguished Teacher of Teachers Award by the University of Wisconsin-Madison. Dr. Johnson has coauthored more than two hundred instructional texts for elementary, middle school, and high school students as well as for adult learners. She has published widely in scholarly journals, and her most recent books are *Wordworks: Exploring Language Play*; *High Stakes: Poverty, Testing, and Failure in American*

Schools; and *Trivializing Teacher Education: The Accreditation Squeeze.* Dr. Johnson earned her Ph.D. at the University of Wisconsin-Madison.

Stephen J. Farenga is professor of human development and learning at Dowling College in Oakdale, New York. His research has appeared in major journals in science education, technology, and education of the gifted. He has also written on the topics of teacher education, accreditation, and standards. Dr. Farenga has taught science for fifteen years at the elementary and secondary levels. He has established an educational research clinic to examine methods of best practice and has served as a consultant for urban and suburban school districts. He is a contributing coeditor of "After the Bell" in the journal *Science Scope;* a contributing author of *Trivializing Teacher Education: The Accreditation Squeeze;* a coauthor of *Knowledge under Construction: The Importance of Play in Developing Children's Spatial and Geometric Thinking;* and is coeditor of the *Encyclopedia on Education and Human Development.* Dr. Farenga earned his Ed.D. from Columbia University.

Daniel Ness is associate professor of human development and learning at Dowling College, where he specializes in the areas of cognitive development, mathematics curriculum, and mathematics instruction. He has taught mathematics at all levels, and has widely practiced assessment techniques—such as naturalistic observation and the clinical method—for diagnosing mathematical thinking and cognition. Dr. Ness is the author of numerous articles on mathematics cognition and the development of spatial and geometric thinking. He is a contributing editor to the column "After the Bell" in *Science Scope;* a contributing author to *Trivializing Teacher Education: The Accreditation Squeeze;* a coauthor of *Knowledge under Construction: The Importance of Play in Developing Children's Spatial and Geometric Thinking;* and coauthor of the *Encyclopedia of Education and Human Development.* Dr. Ness earned his Ph.D. from Columbia University.